SILENCE
BREAKS

SILENCE
BREAKS

book

one

ASHLEE BIRK

Cover and Interior Design: Kathryn Campbell

"The Moments We Stand" logo and cover background by Hannah Craner

The Moments We Stand: Silence Breaks

Print Edition ISBN: 978-0-9904810-0-3

MOBI Edition ISBN: 978-0-9904810-1-0

EPUB Edition ISBN: 978-0-9904810-2-7

Library of Congress Control Number: 2014912043

Printed in the United States of America by CreateSpace

DEDICATION

THIS BOOK IS DEDICATED TO MY BABIES. It is for them that I write. I pray that every word will become a source of love, support, encouragement, and strength that they can carry with them throughout their lives...and hold onto when I am one day gone. When it is my turn to leave this world, I want no word left unsaid. So until then...I write my thoughts, I write of my pain, and I keep a log of the faith and hope that have become a part of me. This is a book about the trials we have overcome together.

I know that because of Jesus Christ, all the roads we have traveled have been blessed with love. I love you kids with all of my heart. I know that without you, I am nothing, because it is *you* who have made me who I am today: a mother...your mother. One day, my dear children, you will be where I am. You will be parents. It will not always be easy. You will have your own trials, and you will have days when you will wonder how you will possibly make it. You will have moments when you won't know where to turn. Remember that we have been there before; we held hands and together, we became stronger during those moments. Trials will come and they will be hard, but do not lose your faith. Have courage and hope that all things will work out for your good if you are true to yourself and to your values.

To every mother who seeks hope for her children...and to every child who has lost hope in the future...you *can* make it! Reach for the ones who lift you up; turn to Christ and find the light that only *He* can bring. No matter where you stand in those moments of fear and pain...you are not alone if you let *Him* steer your course. I know this is true, for I have seen it in the little moments and the big hurdles of my life. To rise above your trials, you must seek for power greater than any you have alone. Stand strong in those difficult moments in which you find yourself, and let a power greater than your own carry you when all you feel capable of doing is falling, for those are the moments when you must STAND.

INTRODUCTION

I BELIEVE IN JESUS CHRIST. I BELIEVE He is the source of truth for this world. I believe that He came to earth and died for us, so that we can one day live again. *He* is my source of higher power. He has given me strength when my own has not been enough. He has been a light for me through some really dark days. I will be referring to Him and the foundation He has been in my life. I ask you to read about what I have learned and apply these truths to your own life. Whether or not you believe in Jesus Christ, or in Heavenly Father, whatever your source of higher power may be, I want you to seek it and the strength that can come from finding power from something beyond yourself. I will refer to Christ as my source of that power.

As you ponder about who or what it is that has been your source of strength, peace, and light in this troubled world, I hope you feel of that spirit as I tell my story of the times when I was carried by a higher power to a brighter road. I believe in the strength that can come when we seek it. I believe in a power that is sometimes inexplicable with the knowledge that we, as human beings, have. I know that each of us is a loved son or daughter of God. I see Him in each person I have ever met, regardless of the life they have chosen or are choosing to live. I know that we must put our trust in Him, and that all we do in this life is possible because of Him.

There is also darkness in this world. I have felt it myself, and seen it in others on many occasions. I know that it is very powerful as well. It has shaken the faith of numerous individuals, some of whom I love with all my heart. I have watched it destroy many families. It is real. It can be scary. I believe that this power's source is Satan. I believe he is the father of all lies and all darkness. He wants us to fail. He delights in our pain. He wants us to curse God. He has one mission . . . to get as many souls to fall as he can. It is his extreme darkness unleashed on the world that brought me to the low points in my life. I have seen the power of this darkness and personally felt its despair. I know it is real.

Yet through all the darkness, I have also seen much light. I have felt the power of light that can become even stronger than any dark day if we will turn toward it. I have felt peace come when it felt impossible. I have been carried higher when I wasn't sure if I would ever see hope again. This is my story. It is one of how darkness can be made light. It is a story of hope.

CONTENTS

Stand Tall: You Are Not Alone

IN LIFE, WE ARE ALL CONSTANTLY AT crossroads. Some of these crossroads are life-changing, and others don't seem to make a difference either way. These moments come to us sometimes many times a day. Which way to choose…what choice to make. Do I take back this lipstick that had dropped behind my purse at the store and now I'm loading all my groceries in the car and I am in a hurry and need to leave? Do I wait at the cross walk with the little boy who looks lost…even though I'm already running late to take my daughter to her piano lesson? It is a moment for a young high school girl when she has to decide if she will walk past the young boy who just got his binder torn out of his hands and his stuff thrown about the hallway…or if she will stop and help him pick it up and be late for her next class. It is the moment when a young man sits in a dressing room contemplating walking out of the store with the T-shirt he just put on under his clothes…or if he takes it off and saves his money to buy it when he can afford it. A young pregnant mother sits at a crossroad at the abortion clinic. . . contemplating whether or not she keeps this unborn child or walks out of there today as if nothing ever happened.

Crossroads are always in our lives. They are sometimes small…and other times very large and heavy. They come to young and old, poor and rich, happy and depressed. We cannot always control when or how they come. The only part we have control over, is the outcome. The outcome of any crossroad can be very dark... or it can bring so much joy for generations to come. We will not always know the ripple effect that our decisions can have on others around us, but sometimes, our decisions will change another person's life forever.

My name is Ashlee. I am a victim of murder. Through a series of events and by two shots of a gun, I was made a widow at the age of 28, with my youngest child just six weeks old. I am a victim of infidelity. I have felt unlovable. I have felt rejected. I have had days in my life when I wasn't sure if I would ever take a breath again, let alone be able to raise my five children by myself. I have lived in fear. I have felt much heartache. I have felt truly broken to my core. I have carried some heavy burdens... not only of my own, but burdens put upon my shoulders by the death of my husband. I have felt alone. I have felt humiliated. I have been humbled to my knees. I have searched my soul to find my worth in this world, and in the life that was left for me. My world has been totally shattered. I have faced realities I never knew were possible, and found strength within myself to keep up the fight and live every day as if it was on purpose. I have been carried by Angels... both earthly beings and those unseen. I have found that being a "victim" doesn't mean we have an excuse to stop living. Being a victim means finding a reason for seeking a higher road. I have picked up the pieces left and carried on. I am a mother. I am a survivor.

In one way or another, we are all victims. There are times in our lives when we are forced to question who we are at our core. When we are presented with a path... we can go this way or we can choose that way. For some, this moment comes when the one person whom we love the most decides we are not enough. This person leave us—at a most vulnerable moment—alone to search within ourselves for who we really are. We are left trying to find who it is that was left behind. Sometimes the person we love dies. Sometimes it is merely an internal battle we are facing...all alone inside our minds. Whatever the situation and wherever you have been...you have been hurt. You have felt alone. You have been abandoned, either by your parents, your lover, your friends, complete strangers, or even yourself. We have all been at that crossroad where all we have left is ourselves.

Sometimes these moments of lows have brought you to your knees and caused you to reflect and ponder your relationship with God...and other times they have made you question if He is even there, or if He knows you are alone. Whatever that moment has been for you, it is personal and real. It has defined and refined who you are, who you think you were, and who you want to become.

This is my story...the defining moments that have truly brought me to my knees, the times when I've questioned to my core my very existence, and the experiences I've had that have shown me who I really am and who my Heavenly Father still needs me to become. The night of my husband's death was my darkest hour, but also the very moment when I saw firsthand that my Heavenly Father sent Angels on errands for me. He carried me. It was the hour when all my fears and all the pain of this world collided together and He was there...putting back together all the pieces, one step at a time.

CHAPTER ONE

Silence Breaks

WHEN EMMETT LEFT THAT NIGHT, I SOMEHOW knew this time was different. He left just as he had on many nights, saying he was going to go run an errand and be right back…but then not coming home for seven or eight hours. I knew in my heart that—just as the previous weeks had shown me—he wasn't coming back any time soon. My six-week old baby began to cry the minute the garage door shut, just as he had done every night. This time, his cry seemed to be a panic, which I not only felt in his screams, but in my heart.

I called Emmett to beg him to come back…no answer. I said a prayer…I pleaded that the nightmares I had been having all week about my baby dying would just go away. This could *not* be the answer the universe had to get this father to realize what he had been given in this life! I prayed that the death of his child would not be the thing that shook his world and helped him want to come home to us. I pleaded with my Heavenly Father that he would not take my baby. I begged that Emmett would be given a chance to find peace and come home to us, and that he would be released from this torment that was plaguing his mind and his choices. I could feel his internal battle of something being wrong. I never heard it from his mouth, but I could see it all over his face. I pleaded that this feeling of panic I had would be calmed tonight, and that whatever it took for Emmett to come home and be the father I needed him to be…would happen. Maybe he could just get arrested and sit in jail for a few nights…

thinking of his amazing life. Maybe he would want to come home to live it. Maybe he could get in a wreck and sit in a hospital bed, finding a realization that his wife and children were worth it...worth taking care of, and that it was worth being his wife's sweetheart and his children's father. At least maybe he could see that it *was* worth coming home to us.

After my prayer, I held my screaming baby in one hand...I held my scriptures in the other hand, and I bounced. For two hours I bounced. My phone sat nearby...silent. Bouncing...screaming...tears rolling down my cheeks. Something was *so* wrong. At about ten p.m., I was overcome by sheer panic. I called and texted him many times. No response. But how was this different than the hundreds of times he had ignored my pleas? Two more hours: bouncing...waiting...crying...panic...reading...singing to my hysterical infant. Would he ever stop crying? Midnight. Baby stopped crying and fell asleep.

Now what? Now I was really alone and the pain sank even deeper in my empty heart. I went to reach for my phone...who could I call? Emmett wouldn't answer. What would I say to my Mom, or my sisters? Would anyone believe me? Something was wrong...I had been saying it for months. No one really seemed to believe me. I finally decided to lie down and try to sleep. My head hit my pillow, but the tears just slid down my face. I guess I kind of knew in my heart that someone was on the way to tell me he had been in a wreck and I could go see him...or that he had been in a fight and I could go bail him out of jail. At least he would be forced to need me. At least I could look him in the eye and tell him I was here for him...and maybe for once in all these crazy months, he would hear me. Maybe this time, he would be in a place to feel our love pouring out all over him.

One a.m....knock...knock...knock. I had fallen asleep. I don't know how, but now I was jolted awake in a dreamy fog. Was all this real? Yes, and it was all going to be okay...right? Yes. Everything would be fine. Right? Each step to the door felt heavier and heavier, and my heart was racing like I had just run a thousand miles. Door opens...three people I had never seen before. Asked if I was Emmett's wife...asked to come in. "NO! I don't know you...just tell me where he is so I can go talk to him!" Ma'am...please let us in..."NO! I am here alone with my five babies, and I don't want you in my house. Just tell me!" "Please Ashlee...please . . ." My sister Ali pulls up to the house...a true inspiration on the part of her boyfriend who had a strong feeling that she needed to head over to my house. Ali was here, I was going to be okay. "Fine...come in! Now tell me where he is." "We need you to sit down . . ." I don't want to freaking sit...Okay. We all sit down around my couch, everyone is fidgeting and they won't look me in the eye. "Ma'am...there has been an accident... and your husband was killed at the Walgreens on Linder."

Heart stops...lungs stop...body freezes. "Kandi...Rob...murdered... affair...gun...Kandi...Emmett...relationship...dead...murdered... Kandi...Rob...gun...Emmett...dead...husband...gone...father of five... murdered...family...broken...life...stopped...adultery...lies...secrets... secret life...murdered...gone...widow...alone...secrets...dead..."

"Kandi...Emmett...found...dead...babies...fatherless..."

I don't remember a single word, just phrases and pieces. I couldn't breathe. My heart was pounding into my lungs and my lungs were full of all the lies, all the secrets that were finally being told to me. And now he was gone. No 'I am sorry's'. No: 'Please forgive me's.' Nothing but emptiness, humiliation, and utter despair. He was gone: the man to whom I had promised to stick with it through the good and the bad. Now, I had all the answers as to why it was going so badly, and he wasn't even here to work with me to make it all right.

All I could think about was our five babies sleeping soundly in their beds, having no idea that their universe had just been shattered. Where would I even begin? Could I just lie to them? Could I cover up all the bad stuff and just say he got in a car wreck? NO. That would just be more lies. Lies are what got us here in the first place. Plus, if they didn't hear it from me, they would hear it from friends or read it on the Internet one day, then look back and think *I* was the liar. But how could I let them hear this? Me, a mother who hated my kids to even play with toy guns, a mother who skipped over the word 'killed' or 'dead,' or 'murdered' in our scriptures. And now their super hero— the man who was supposed to always protect them and keep them safe—had been brutally gunned down because he was sleeping with another man's wife. How could I change that story to protect my innocent babies' minds?

That night was filled with these questions and turmoil inside myself. I wanted to be able to protect this man whom I had loved for seven years. I wanted to be able to just take away all the pains that would follow that black night. But that is not how this world works. We have to face truths, we have to be strong for our babies, we have to have faith that even on the worst night of our lives, our Heavenly Father is going to carry us through —carry us through in the words we have to speak, carry us through the painful truths, and carry us through to keep taking another breath... keeping us moving forward and living...not only for ourselves but for the ones who need us.

I remember walking into my closet that night to beg Heavenly Father for a 'do over.' I begged Him for answers to why all of this was real. I fell to my knees and pleaded for the peace that I needed. The most peaceful feeling came over my body. A still, small voice whispered to my heart: "BE STILL...I have been here, and I am still here. Angels have guarded this home and each of you. None of that has changed. It will be hard, but you have to keep moving forward. You have to have faith for a brighter day, which will come as long as you keep protecting these sweet children and having faith in Me. You are *not* alone. You have been watched over, and I am proud of you. I *believe* in you. Now is the time when you have to decide if your testimony has been in your perfect life and your husband, or if your testimony is in Me. Ashlee, be still. Breath. You did all you could. You did your best. I am so proud of you. You were an amazing wife; you are an incredible mother. You are still you. Do not let this define who you will become. You are still the Ashlee you have always been, and I see so much good in you. Believe in yourself and do not doubt who you are because of the pain you now feel so deeply. Find forgiveness and peace. This is the time to find the beauty that is still all around you. Make the world a better place for those children I have blessed you with. *I* will carry you when it gets unbearable, but I need *you* to STAND."

And there it was…the defining moment I was praying so hard for *Emmett* to receive. The moment when you realize that all you have and all you are doing is worth it because Heavenly Father is proud of you. *He* is the reason you have been given all that you have. Why we couldn't have had that moment together, I will never know for sure, but I understood that the "Why" in life was sometimes not always answered. It is the "How" in life we have to seek. How can I show my Father in Heaven that I believe Him when He said He watched over me and has been with me? I can keep living, and move forward. He asked me that night to be more than just me…He asked me to believe in *Him* and have faith that *He* would be there to help me through it all. And day by day, He gave me opportunities to accomplish things and to continue to find ways to do all that He asked of me. That night, He asked me to have faith, but then, He not only gave me the courage to follow that faith, He laid out before me the path that would bring me the peace and healing He desired for me. Peace and healing has come in a series of moments…one step at a time.

Heavenly Father loves each one of us individually, regardless of the choices we make. He sees our worth as a person no matter who we are. He saw the beauty of all the letters sent to us to brighten our days. He saw all the times people dropped by to take my kids to a movie or a hockey game. He saw every floor that was mopped and toilet that was cleaned. He saw all the closets in my house that were organized, and the meals brought in with love. He saw the checks that were written. He read the emails that gave me strength. He witnessed the blankets that were sewn for my babies out of their daddy's clothes. Not one good deed we do on this earth goes unnoticed. Even though, at times, we all feel a little invisible…He is always there. He sends his love in ways that we don't always realize come from Him. And sometimes, He uses us to be someone else's Angel. Each one of us was made just the way we are…on purpose.

I think the moment I truly understood unconditional love was when we were sitting in Rob's murder trial. For three weeks, we all sat there: Emmett's family on one side, and Rob's on the other. We all listened to the facts. We all knew exactly what happened. The facts were the facts. I watched his family. I watched his Mother. She loves her son. She is aware of the fact that he isn't perfect, and that he made a life-altering decision, and yet her love for him as her son lives on. That is how I see our Father viewing all of us. We all make mistakes. Some of them are life-changing, and some of them will never be known by anyone else…and yet our Heavenly Father loves us still. He sees our worth, He finds good in us. We are still His son or daughter.

Whatever path has led you down roads you wish you could change, there is still hope. You can find a way back to the road you always dreamed of as a kid. You can be anything you want to be. Our past does not have to define our future. We have the power to make a change. We can become whoever we choose to be. Nobody can tell you that you do not have worth, because no matter who you are…you do.

I don't think I truly knew that until all the things that gave me a sense of self-worth were taken away. Find your sense of worth by being the best person you can be. Find it by writing letters to someone in their need. Find it in serving someone else. Find it by becoming selfless and living your life to make your Heavenly Father proud of you, because every other outside source powering your view of your self-worth can literally be taken away in a second. All that we have in our lives is because of Jesus Christ. *He* is the reason for every blessing. So let us live each moment in gratitude for the fragile blessings we all have.

CHAPTER TWO

Angels

I THINK I WAS IN SHOCK LITERALLY from the moment those words hit my ears until long after the funeral a week later. There are parts of days of which I literally have no memory whatsoever. Living in shock is an out-of-body experience. Sometimes looking back, I am still not entirely sure if that was even really me, or a bad movie.

I do remember the clock ticking closer and closer to seven a.m. that next morning and dreading hearing footsteps on the stairs. I knew my children would wake up as usual...like on a normal morning. I knew I had a big job to do. By the time morning came, my house was filled with family and friends. Many of them had received texts or calls in the middle of their sleep, and got in their cars to drive hours through the night.

When the sounds of my little ones did come, my body hurt. How could any mother do this? I was frozen inside. All five kids came and sat down on the couch, in the same place where I had sat just hours before. But this time, *I* was on the other end. This time, *I* was the one looking around the room trying hard not to make eye contact with them.

Surrounded by family and with the help of my bishop, we taught them about Heaven. I held baby Tytus in my arms and we talked about how he had just come down from Heaven to join our family just six short weeks earlier. My bishop wore a glove on his hand. We told them that there had been an accident and that—just like when you take a glove off your hand—Daddy Emmett's spirit had gone back to that place from which Tytus had just come. Daddy was no longer on this earth any more. He was now with Heavenly Father and Jesus.

Their eyes pierced my soul. I could see utter despair and panic stirring in their little minds. The oldest of the twins began to cry hysterically. The other kids didn't move. They just sat there looking at me with the same look I felt…"What are we supposed to do now?"

Night came again. I had now been awake for forty-eight hours, and my body showed no signs of letting sleep set in ever again. I remember crying so hard that night in my mother's arms that I don't think one ounce of liquid was left in my entire body. She just held me while I sobbed. I would stop and punch my pillow as if maybe it could take all the pain out of my body. Then I would sob some more. It seemed that every emotion was attacking my heart. The sadness would hit…then the anger would take over again. It was like a ship being tossed to and fro in the ocean; back and forth.

The easy part was the anger, because then I didn't have to miss him. I tried hard to keep my mind there…focusing on just those last months we had experienced together. The anger allowed every good memory to disappear and only the pain to have a voice. I felt safe when the anger had the power. It was when the despair would roll in that it was almost more than I could bear. Memories of the life we had created. Thoughts about the dreams we had once shared; reality that I now had to make those dreams come true without him. Sleep finally came, and within what seemed like minutes, I was awake again.

The next morning is one that I remember as if it all happened yesterday. I know at some point I was awake in the night to feed the baby, but the only thing that woke me up that morning was the muffled sounds of my children's voices. It was a faint noise, and I couldn't make out anything they were saying.

My heart was racing and I felt out of my body. I was foggy and shaky, and I felt like the world around me should have no right to keep turning.

The morning before, I had sat my children down to tell them that their dad had been shot and killed. This morning, I had nothing left. I peeled myself out of bed and opened my bedroom door. The house was dark, but I could see the outline of my four oldest children sitting around the kitchen table with a big box right in the center. They were frantically writing on papers and throwing them inside the box. "What are you guys doing?" I asked. My oldest daughter, Bailey, paused for only a second, long enough to look up at me and say, "Mom...yesterday there was a tsunami in Japan. Grandma told us that lots of little boys and girls lost their moms and dads...and we are sending them this package to help them know that they are loved and that we are praying for them."

I grabbed some of their letters and, with tears rolling down my face, I read a few out loud: "I know you feel sad, but Heavenly Father loves you. We are praying for you." "You will see your dad again someday." "I wish I could take the pain away." "You are loved."

These children were in the darkest hour they had ever known...and yet they weren't sitting around feeling sorry for themselves. How could this be? They were reaching out to comfort others who were in pain. That day, they were a light for me.

That moment and that box were one of the greatest blessings of strength I could have ever received. That was the moment when I knew I had little Angels in my home to help lead the way for me to find a higher road and press on until we could breathe again.

For anyone else who has ever felt Angels—seen or unseen— standing in their presence...it is a tender mercy sent straight from God. I knew I had to keep moving—despite the fact that my soul had almost had more than it could take—even if it was THEIR faith that would sometimes be what carried us.

It is when we cannot do it anymore that He sends us such blessings. This life is so hard at times, but I am so thankful for the little boxes and blessings that can be a beacon of light to help us find our way.

What is the purpose of life? The purpose of life is to become like Christ through a series of tests that can, at times, make us want to abandon Him entirely. It is to find the blessings when some might find only a curse. This life is to help us find our strengths when we are constantly bombarded with weaknesses, temptations, trials, and pain. It's to find joy in the little things. This life is for us to come to see that all we have is *Him*. No matter where we are, what we have, or what we have lost, Christ has felt our pain. He knows our name, and He hears our prayers. This life is just a blink in the eternal path we are trying to navigate, but it is that blink that will determine where our hearts long to be when we die. It is during these brief moments that we will prove our testimonies. We have this chance to show God that we will be strong in our faith, no matter what blocks our path. We will be diligent to the missions He sent us here to fulfill. The purpose of this life is to discover where He wants us to be, and to learn to find joy wherever we are. And when we are able to do this, nothing Satan throws our way will ever cause us to forget who carried us through the darkness.

CHAPTER THREE

What is Forgiveness?

WHAT IS FORGIVENESS? FOR ME, IT HAD always been an exchange of words: a mutual agreement after a wrong had been done that all was forgiven. My life had been filled with moments where I or someone else had to ask for forgiveness—and it always felt like an easy thing to do. In the past, when I heard those sweet words, there was never a doubt that I would forgive the person and move on. I felt I had mastered the art of forgiveness at every opportunity that had presented itself, and now here I was…left with three people I knew I had to forgive. Only this time, contrary to everything I had experienced up to this point, I was never going to hear from any of them that they were sorry. Emmett was gone. His chance to ever say the words I needed to hear was gone. And the other two…well, I barely knew them.

Some months earlier, as summer turned to fall, Emmett finally passed the bar. He started talking about a paralegal he was going to hire. She wanted him to start his own criminal defense firm and she had offered to come and lead his team. He said she wouldn't be able to start until after Christmas because she had to wait to get her giant Christmas bonus, so she would just be sending him clients under the table from the firm where she currently worked.

Red flags started going off like sirens in my mind! I immediately thought back to my single years, dating guys who were still technically dating someone else but who were trying to get me to secretly date them on the side. Emmett told me the paralegal had been treated badly by her boss and she wanted him to file a lawsuit against him for maltreatment of her and other former employees. She also told Emmett she needed protection from her husband, who was verbally, emotionally, and physically abusive. She wanted Emmett's protection and help in finding a good divorce attorney.

"She is an older lady," he told me. "She is like a mother figure to me. She really believes in me and says I'm an amazing attorney." It sounded like trouble to me, and I told him exactly how I felt about it. If anyone was going to come work for us, I wanted to make sure we did it the right way, and had no baggage that could get us into a sticky situation. My questioning didn't go over well. Looking back, I realize I shouldn't have given up so easily...because that feeling that came into my heart was completely accurate. This woman—who professed to be so picked on and abused—would not only come to work for my husband...she would change my life forever.

Well, as good bosses tend to do, the paralegal's employer figured out that she had been sending his clients to Emmett and he fired her. In a matter of hours...she had landed her new employment at Emmett's bankruptcy office. And so began their criminal law office. I think I got a phone call from Emmett saying, "Well Kandi got fired...She is starting today and I am going to make *a lot* of money with her here." Money—a very overrated replacement for relationships and love. A necessity I learned to despise. And they did. They started bringing in a lot of money.

One day, I had a doctor's appointment downtown, and I decided to go surprise Emmett in hopes that he had a minute to take me to lunch—something we had never done since our move to our new town. I pulled into the parking lot behind the office. Directly behind Emmett's truck was *her* car. It was parked at an angle, almost touching his. I remember just staring at it. In hind sight, it was like she had parked behind him, as if to say..."I own you now. You don't leave the office until I do." Her license plate read 'Kandi's.' I got a pit in my stomach. I hobbled my pregnant belly up the ramp and walked back towards Emmett's office. Everyone was looking at me as if I were wearing no clothes. Was I missing something?

Emmett's office door was shut. I was about to knock when one of the secretaries said, "He is in there with Kandi. I dare you to just walk in!" And so I did. They were giggling, and then turned and looked at me as if I were a ghost. That was the first time I met Kandi. She had on a miniskirt and hooker boots. Her cleavage was everywhere! She *was* older... she looked like she was being paid for her "not-so-professional" services. I felt nauseous. I felt she was definitely not the type of woman to whom Emmett would be attracted. She *was* older... and that was reassuring to my poor mind that had been playing tricks on me at an incredible rate since hearing about this situation. I felt like a crazy person! One minute, my heart would tell me they were having an affair... and then my logic would kick in and calm down my nerves. *"She is old. ...You are a great mother and wife. He loves you....You are the one who is the mother of his soon-to-be five children. You have always given him everything when it came to being intimate. ...You are enough. You are encouraging and supportive.... Why on earth would he want her?"*

And so began my many months of this internal battle. I knew she was no good, and yet...I believed every word I heard about her from Emmett; but I entertained every doubt that bubbled up inside of me and that inner instinct was like a fire ready to ignite. Something wasn't quite right.

Kandi and I met on a few other occasions, mainly when I showed up at the office. One time, after the baby was born, she even held him. He had just fallen asleep in his car seat, and I really wanted to just show him to everyone. Emmett was adamant that she hold him. She sent Emmett home with beautiful gifts: blankets and outfits for the baby, and even a care package for me. She even offered to babysit him so the rest of us could go to a movie. That was an idea I quickly squelched because of my internal battle about whether she really was just a kind, older woman who believed in Emmett … or if she was trying to destroy my family. She was always kind. She even sent me thank you notes on Facebook for her Christmas present.

I had no obvious reason to doubt Emmett's assurance that she was an amazing paralegal who would make him lots of money and help him start his business.

Now for Rob. I had only actually heard his name one time before March 11, 2011. It was just a few weeks earlier, on our way back from the movie when Kandi had insisted on babysitting Tytus. All seven of us were in the car. Emmett had posted something on Facebook about a run-in with a Californian…"who could talk big…but couldn't walk the walk." I asked him about it. He said that it was Kandi's husband, Rob…"who needed to get a clue." I finally asked a question for which I had wanted an answer for a long time. I said, "I understand that you are worried about an employee, but why is it your job to protect her?" He didn't answer right away. I am sure he was debating in his mind what the real answer was, and what the answer he wanted *me* to hear was going to be. All he said was, "Well someone has got to."

As a person, Emmett was a protector. He was an amazing friend, and would always have anyone's back. That was one of his qualities that caused me to fall in love with in him. And yet, in that moment, my heart wanted to pound out of my chest. I felt a panic, as if there were more to this story about these people. He didn't want to talk about it anymore. So, I was left to hallucinate in my mind the 'whats' and the 'whys' to try to make sense of it all.

Rob Hall. I knew his name, but I had never seen his face. Then, for the year and a half after March 11, Rob Hall was just a mug shot in my mind. A mug shot I would scream at while driving alone in my car. A picture I would silently talk to every morning as I sat alone in my bathroom doing my make-up. For a year and half, while awaiting the trial, his mug shot silently consumed me. I saw him…or her…in every store I entered, and in almost every person I passed. I scanned the room in restaurants before sitting down to order my food. I looked out every window I walked past at my home...searching for that mug shot, expecting him to be pointing his gun at me.

Three people; three different crossroads that had all collided and exploded. Everywhere we go, we meet people. Each of them different. Our paths cross, sometimes without a sound. And other times, as they cross, they destroy our paths and leave a hole. We aren't really given a map of where to go in life, but we are given those feelings inside. Those deeply rooted impressions that something is not quite right. I never got answers about those feelings, until after the explosion—probably because I was naïve...but mainly because I didn't believe in myself. I doubted impressions that possibly could have made a difference.

As I knelt in my closet that night after Emmett's death, I thought the answer to my prayer was that I had forgiven each of them—like putting a check on a list of the things Heavenly Father was asking me to do. I thought for sure, if He was asking right then...that I could accomplish said check marks the moment I knew I had to let it go. Little did I know that my pain and my anger and my need to forgive would literally start eating me alive.

CHAPTER FOUR

Whispers of Love

IT WAS CRAZY THAT DURING THE VERY week when all I wanted to do was lie in bed in the fetal position—and try to figure out where to begin to grieve—I also had an endless list of responsibilities to accomplish. I felt like I didn't even have a minute to sit down and think, which at the time, I hated. However, looking back, that lack of time to think probably saved my life. I had to do the normal stuff that needs to be done when a person passes away: calls to phone companies to turn off Emmett's—and ironically Kandi's—cell phones. Meetings with bankers to try to figure out the best way to create bank accounts to allow me to be the representative to pay off clients whose cases were not complete. Meetings with the office to try to decide who and what individuals needed their money back. Cleaning out Emmett's office. Meeting with the mortuary to plan the funeral.

Then I had a separate list of responsibilities that had to do with the murder investigation. Meetings with detectives. Answering questions about everything I knew. I wanted them to have every piece of information I could give them. I wanted the truth to be told, so that they had everything they needed to do their job to the very best of their abilities. I told them every detail of my side of the story, and everything I knew about the three individuals involved.

It was like being in a dream when I walked into the mortuary. I ordered the programs, picked out the casket and flowers. I kind of sat there pretending like I was an actress, and that this wasn't really happening. I had a lump in my throat the entire time we were there. My stepfather drove me home, and tears just slid down my cheek. How was this real? I couldn't plan a funeral! I wouldn't! On that drive home, I made up my mind to just pretend that it wasn't real, and to procrastinate long enough for someone else to come plan the funeral for me. I felt that if I could just ignore it…then maybe it all wouldn't be real. I wasn't able to deal with the finality of deciding who would speak, and who would say the closing prayer. I wasn't going to do it, and that was final.

We walked into the house. I went into my room to feel sorry for myself for a little bit. I lay down on my bed. Tears welled up in my eyes and slid down, soaking my pillow. All of the sudden, I got this strong impression. GRAB A PEN. I grabbed a paper and a pen and I started to write. Within about five minutes, every detail of the funeral was written down on my paper. Every name of the pallbearers, every speaker, and the order of those who would speak. Even down to who would dedicate the grave. I didn't do any of it. My pen just wrote, as I continued to sob.

I walked out of my room to type up my husband's funeral. As I read it out loud, I felt the spirit so strongly. It was exactly how Emmett would have wanted it. It all made sense. He knew I couldn't do this job by myself…so he did it for me.

The day of the viewing arrived. My biggest fear was that Kandi would show up—that she would try to come and steal yet another day from me. It consumed me as I got ready. At one point, I had thought the viewing should be closed-casket because of the location of the bullet holes, but with make-up, the morticians had done an amazing job with his appearance.

I got there early to have some time alone with him. I yelled. I cried. Alone in a room with a body. How did we get here? Why did this have to be the end of everything on which I had worked so hard? I am not sure how long I spent in there, and I have no idea of who could hear me. It felt good to shout at him. It felt good to tell him how mad I was that he had put me through all of this. I blamed him for the hours I had spent that week with detectives instead of with our children. I wanted to hit him. I wanted to hold him. I wanted to shake him and tell him that he couldn't do this to me. He couldn't leave me alone! He had promised to help me throughout this life. He had promised to take care of me. He had promised me that we would have it all.

The viewing began. I was still alone. His family members began trailing in the room. Some were mad and yelled at me for having the casket open. Others wouldn't come talk to me. All of us were dealing with our emotions in our own ways. They huddled in a corner, so I stood by his casket alone. People began to trickle in. No one really knew what to say. Everyone was crying. Not me. I somehow believed that I had to be strong for all these people who had come to say goodbye to their friend, their neighbor, their boss, their cousin, their son. I thought that maybe if I could be strong, they could all make it though their own grief. Then in walked my mom. She ran over and grabbed my hand. My throat burned from holding back tears. I had to fight them off. My face was on fire.

People streamed in from all over. People from our past. People from our current life. Hundreds of hugs. I felt the love and strength each person brought, but I wasn't about to show them I was weak. I was in zombie mode. I wasn't comforting anyone … I was a stone wall. My friend Lyric had collected pictures and made a video to some of our favorite songs. All of the sudden, they turned it on … and that's when the dam burst. My tears didn't just start sliding down my face—they poured. All the emotion that had been bottled inside me up to this point came flying out. Now as I hugged people, I actually let them in. I needed them. Each hug spoke to my soul. You are loved. You can do this. We are here for you. And my soul began to speak back. I am thankful for your love. I need you. Thanks for being here for me today.

I wasn't alone. I had thousands of people who believed in me. I had so many who came because they loved me. They loved Emmett. They loved these kids.

I had the kids stay in the playroom so people could go see them after they visited with Emmett. I didn't want them to see their Dad this way. A decision I would later question…but what I felt at that time was the best decision. When the viewing was over and the casket was closed, we brought in the kids. I don't know that they totally comprehended what it was we were doing. They just wanted to touch the casket and try to look inside. Everyone in the room just stopped and watched them. The children were tender as they whispered to the box. They whispered about memories. They talked about love.

In our faith, soon after a baby is born, the father gives that child a name and blessing, something Emmett had not had the opportunity to do. So, I asked my brother Jeff to bless Tytus. A huge group of men came and surrounded the casket. With Emmett in the middle of it all, Jeff gave Tytus the blessing his father couldn't. It was a tender moment for me. I don't think it made sense to anyone else, but for me it was beautiful. It allowed Emmett to be a part of one last thing with our baby boy: the baby he would never see take his first bite of food or first steps. He would miss it all.

No one seemed to want to leave. We all just kind of stood there waiting. The funeral director finally ushered everyone out to their cars. I don't think anyone knew what to do with themselves.

One thing I remember about that night was my stepsister Rachel playing with my hair. I just laid myself face down on my couch and she ran her fingers threw my hair…over and over. It was the first time all week that I actually felt relaxed, like I was in another place. The tears still flowed, but for once I wasn't thinking at all.

I had many family members staying with me that night, but my tears didn't stop until long after they had gone to bed and were asleep. I sat in my room wide-eyed. I wondered how I would handle another day of tears. I wondered how the funeral would go the next day. I didn't know how I could possibly be strong enough to take this another day. I had to make it through one more day…just one more day.

CHAPTER FIVE

The Truth Will Set You Free

THE FUNERAL TOOK PLACE ON MARCH 17, 2011: St. Patrick's Day. Emmett loved that holiday. His ancestors were from Ireland, and he was named after one of them. So it didn't surprise me that it was the day on which we celebrated Emmett's life.

I woke up that morning in hopes that the night before had all been a bad dream. It hadn't. The limo driver from the funeral home came to pick us up. All the kids piled in, excited to ride in a limo for the first time. My mother rode with us.

The limo driver started to drive towards the church where the funeral was to take place. My heart started to pound. He was taking the route that would pass by Walgreens. I hadn't yet been able to drive by, and I wasn't about to have the trip to the funeral be the first time. I started having a panic attack, and I just stared at my mom. She could tell exactly what I was thinking. She gestured up to the driver and asked him if he could turn around and go the long way to the church. He very patiently apologized, turned around, and took us to the church the long way. The church was busting at the seams. Emmett's popularity and ability to make friends was certainly apparent everywhere I looked. The halls were lined with people.

Family had gathered in the viewing room with the casket. I think shock had given me an adrenaline boost, because today I felt stronger than I anticipated. I had my babies by my side. We walked in and took our place on the front row. Someone came and got Kaleeya to take her to the nursery. I hated to see her go, but I also knew that she would be very distracting and restless. My good friend Brittany had been asked to take Tytus. I wanted them to be in the building, but I didn't want to worry about them during the service. My stepfather said the family prayer in the viewing room before the family members joined the rest of the congregation in the chapel. He was so eloquent with each sentence he spoke. The spirit filled the room, and I had chills all over my body.

They asked us to begin the line to follow the casket into the chapel. It was still bustling with people, and was filled clear to the back. People were even standing in corners because every seat had been taken. I scanned the room to make sure Kandi wasn't anywhere to be seen…a talent I have become skilled at as the years have rolled by. We turned to go down the aisle to our seats when Teage pulled on my hand and said, "I can't do this Mom…I need to leave." I leaned down and gave him a kiss. "I understand buddy. I don't want to do this either." "Mom…I have to go find Kaleeya." So my little boy went to the nursery to join his sister. Later, my friend Emily—who was there with the children—told me that when he was asked if was okay, he said only these few words: "My Daddy is in a box."

Now it was just me and the twins. It felt weird not to be surrounded by all five of my children. I took my seat, with one of my girls on each side of me. I was still feeling pretty strong. I could do this. It was going to be a beautiful service. Emmett's cousins were going to do the life sketch. Our good friend Frank was going to share some memories. Emmett's best friend from high school, Jason, would say the closing prayer. I had two of my babies holding my hands. I could be strong.

The music began…and so did my tears. I was shaking like a dog who just got its first bath. The whole bench felt like an earthquake had just hit. HOW WAS THIS REAL? All the strength that had allowed me to walk into this crowded room of people quickly washed out of me with every tear. My twins glanced at me every few minutes and then looked back down at their laps and silently wept, gripping my hands a little tighter with every glance. By the time the first speaker began, I felt so light-headed that I could hardly breathe. My chest felt heavy, like it did on the night I first heard the news of Emmett's death.

I finally got my body to relax, and I tried to listen to the messages being taught. I prayed for peace so that I would be able to listen and think and remember. The stories told were beautiful. The memories priceless. The love these people had for Emmett illuminated every word said. It was a perfect service, just the way it was supposed to be. At one point, I could hear my baby cry in the back. I knew it was him, and I wanted to just get up and go get him. Later, Brittany told me about her experience with him in the hall. She said she couldn't get him to calm down, and all of the sudden, he stopped crying. He was looking up and smiling like someone was making faces at him. Who knows what Angel was there helping my baby boy be calmed?

The closing song was *God Be With You Till We Meet Again.* My soul ached. The music rocked me, and the message brought hope. That song— which I had heard so many times before—now had so much more meaning to its sweet words.

I didn't want it to end. I wanted to just sit there forever, listening to the words and music of faith. The minute I stood up...I knew that peace would not come so easily. I knew that this moment of calm wouldn't last forever, but it felt safe. Getting up out of my seat would mean that I was ready to put my husband's body into the ground. And I wasn't. Eventually, my aching spirit lost, and I stood up to walk out to greet everyone.

I saw faces I hadn't seen in years. They were beautiful reminders of my past. People from my childhood coming to show support. Friends from all walks of life. Friends of Emmett's whom I had never met before. Love pouring out on us from all over the place.

The luncheon following the funeral was beautiful. Photos were displayed everywhere. My little ones had a chance to prance around the room giving loves. Teage was attached at the hip to my sister's boyfriend, Will. It made me happy to see Teage connect with someone. He was the one I was worried about the most. He had taken this harder than anyone. He had no life in him at all. He just kind of clung to people and wouldn't let anyone go. He was even more of a zombie than I was. His little mind seemed to be constantly racing from scenarios of fear. It wasn't until later that night that I would find out exactly what was going on inside his head.

Let me go back a bit to explain this. One October morning, five months before Emmett's death, the twins were at school, Kaleeya was asleep, and Teage came into my room while I was applying my make-up. "Mom," he said, "remember when I went to the movie *Megamind?*... Dad's friend, Kandi, from his office... she was there."

Pit in stomach..."Oh yeah buddy, that is crazy. Did you guys run into her?" I asked. "No," he replied, "but she was there."

I picked up the phone and called Emmett at work, and after a few minutes I said, "Hey... Teage is talking about Kandi being at the movie with you guys. Did you run into her?" "No..." he answered, "He sat by a lady who kept giving him candy... Let me talk to him."

Teage had his ear to the phone. "Oh... okay," he said, "yeah, yeah, uh huh...."

He hung up the phone. "Mommy, I lied. Kandi was not there, it was just a lady with candy."

After that phone conversation, I thought about that day... Emmett had acted strange. He said he wanted some alone time with Teage and they were going to go to a movie. I had suggested that Kaleeya and I go with them as well, since the twins would be at a friend's birthday party. His reply was an awkward and unexplained, "Hell no!" that left me with an uneasy feeling inside of me.

The night of the funeral, my brother Josh brought over *Megamind* for the kids to watch. I was in packing for our trip the next day to the

cemetery, which was out-of-state. Teage came walking into my room...
and almost word for word, said, "Hey Mom...remember when I went to
Megamind? She really was there, Mom...I LIED to you. WHY did I have
to lie?...WHY was she there? Why did I have to lie to you?"

I dropped my bag and scooped him up. I said, "I know Teage. She was
there, but it is not your fault. You didn't lie to me. There is nothing you did
that could make me stop loving you. Everything is going to be okay." He
cried and cried. He felt guilty. He felt betrayed. He didn't talk much, just
cried in my arms. It was like my arms were excited to hold him and wel-
come him to race. The race to figure out where to begin to grieve. I knew
I wasn't alone. Teage's little mind and heart were in a battle just like mine
were: a battle that would take years to overcome. His confession that day
was just the beginning of deep-rooted fears and secrets that would prevent him from being a little care-free kid.

The decisions we make don't just affect us. In the moment, something
might seem innocent and fun. We only care about ourselves. For some,
these times come many times a day. It is easy to think that we are the exception...that what we do is okay. I don't think Emmett had any clue of
the impact that decision to take Teage to the movies that day would have
on his son months later. And I know Emmett didn't think that his chance
to right that wrong, which he had left for tomorrow to fix, would be taken
away with two shots of a gun.

Teage had been holding in a lie, and now it was time to let it go. Time
to set it free. I was so proud of him. He was honest with me. He was honest with himself. He was a great example to me that night. At four years
old, my boy stood a little taller that day. The truth can set you free. Every time the truth is obscured in darkness...we are letting Satan have the
power. Secrets and deception will never win...though it might seem easy
in a moment of shame...truth will find you. Light will win. In those moments, it is our chance to make sure we are on the team that will always
prevail.

If there is a silent secret inside of you … now is the time to let it go. If you have wronged someone … now is your moment to set it right. All we have is now. If you think you will resolve your situation tomorrow … you just never know if that will be. You have been blessed with this moment NOW. Make it count.

CHAPTER SIX

A Time to Say Goodbye

THE DAY OF EMMETT'S BURIAL FOR ME was the hardest one yet. I am not sure if it was the long drive and the silence in the car...or the fact that I knew the whole way that we were going to put his body in the ground.

The drive was five hours. His family had requested that he be taken to Bear Lake, Utah and I knew that is what he would have wanted. I had totally forgotten to calculate the time to stop and nurse my baby into the drive. I hadn't really had a chance yet to get on a real schedule since he was born. We were already running late. The funeral had been the day before, and my body felt like it weighed a million pounds. I could barely walk, let alone...drive all of my kids and my little sister Abbey five hours in the car.

Why hadn't I changed this in the plan? Why had I thought I could handle three emotional days in a row without a break? I started to wish I had given myself a day after the funeral to rest. We had found out right before the viewing that Kaleeya, who was nineteen months old, had pneumonia so I had left her with my mom and stepdad. I didn't like leaving her or them, but I also didn't like the thought of her getting sicker because of my selfish desire to have her with me.

There was no fog around the car...but the fog in my mind was like a state of darkness. I could not think at all. The roads were a bit snowy, and I am pretty sure if it had been any other day I would have turned around and gone back home. I didn't like the feeling of being out of control in my mind and driving in the bad weather. They were a scary mix for me that day.

I don't remember ever pressing the pedal in the car. I don't remember filling it up with gas. I have no idea if the oil had been changed. I really don't even know if I turned the steering wheel. I don't know if we said any words to each other that whole drive. I still can't recall if the kids even said a word. I know that Angels drove my car that day. They kept the gas tank full. They pushed on the break and the gas... and somehow we made it to Bear Lake.

As we got into town, I could see the rows of trees that Emmett had planted the summer just before we met. He was so proud of those trees. They had grown taller now, and were so full of life. There had never been a time we had passed them that he hadn't told me the whole story about how hard it was to plant them all by himself across the whole field. He had worked for days to make sure the row was straight and each tree was in its right spot. They stood tall, almost mocking me. Reminding me of every time we had laughed as we drove by them.

We pulled into the cemetery about an hour late. I could still see the trees, this time now up on the hill from the cemetery, and the view was spectacular of each tree. Everyone had been standing out in the cold snow for an hour... waiting for us. I had been crying the whole way and my make-up was everywhere. I had planned in my mind that I would be able to change and get presentable... but here we were in sweatshirts and jeans and snow boots. We got out of the car and began trudging in the snow to join the mass of people surrounding the casket.

It was freezing. The snow on the top of each headstone sent a chill down my spine. I wanted to scream. This wasn't real. This wasn't my life. These weren't my kids walking in the cold snow to say one last goodbye to their father. This couldn't be real. This had to be a dream. When was I going to wake up? When was this cold chill going to turn warm again? Everyone was watching us. I hated the stares, and yet I don't know what I would have done without each set of eyes motioning me to keep walking.

One of Emmett's best friends, Casey, dedicated the grave. It was a precious, tender prayer. The bishop there thanked everyone for coming and let us know about a luncheon they had prepared. Then he said we could take a minute alone to say goodbye.

My kids had begged and begged to see his body at the viewing, but I had not let them...a decision I felt strongly about at the time. Because of the bullet hole in his forehead, they had to use so much make-up that it didn't even look like him at all. I, a grown woman, had even wished I would have just let his face be a memory in my mind. Once you see a person as a body, you don't ever forget it. I had hoped the kids would understand my feelings, that they would be able to find peace, and that I had made the right decision for them.

The kids were still pretty upset at me for not letting them "say goodbye." As we walked over to touch the casket one last time, the three oldest began to scream and shout at me. "Mommy...please...open this box!" They crouched down and tried to look inside the cracks. Then they started shouting through the holes, "Daddy! Please wake up...DADDY...please if you can hear us...OPEN THIS BOX! Mommy won't let us say goodbye to you, Daddy. Please Daddy. We need to see your face." I am not sure how long they yelled at me...and at Emmett...to open the box. It felt like a lifetime. They pounded on the top of the casket...sobbing. Their cries pierced my heart. They didn't understand. They thought this moment was something I was keeping from them. All they knew was that their daddy's body was in that box, and I was the one who was keeping it shut.

I felt horrible. I felt like a really bad mom. I was failing them. It had only been one week, and I was already messing up. I was filled with guilt...like somehow, I had done all of this to them. Each pound on the casket was like someone was drilling in my mind the fact that I had not only lost my marriage...but that I was going to lose my babies too. Maybe I should have just let them "say goodbye." Maybe it would have all been easier for them if they had seen his face one last time. I will never know for sure. It has definitely been a tender topic at this house, and a very emotional one for us all.

I don't ever wish this moment on anyone. Burying the body of a soul you love is so hard. And that day, I realized that making decisions that affect others' grieving process was not easy either. These five children depended on me to be strong and help them through the road of healing that had not yet even begun. I still think I made the right decision. I hope that someday, when they look back, they will be able to see that I did what I thought was best for them.

I remember that afternoon, Emmett's cousin, Angie, saying, "It's a pretty crazy club we belong to." She was referring to the death of her mother and other loved ones that had impacted all of our lives. That was an eyeopener for me.

We are all going to lose things we love. Death is inevitable. It is a constant—which in one way or another— we will all face. It is a club for everyone who has lost a loved one. It is a feeling you only understand when your roadmap of life presents it to you. It can come on any day and in any

way. It comes to us all. The only thing that is not certain is when it will come. When will the last talk we have with our parents be? When will our last kiss with the ones we love be? When will we, ourselves, take our last breaths? We will never know until that time comes.

That truth is one that has made me really ponder who I want to be in life. When I stand at those crossroads…those moments when we must choose a path…I can tell you with all my heart that the finality of death will be in the back of my mind as I make my decisions. I will pray for guidance that my choices will be those of virtue…that my legacy will be one of honor. Death will come to us all. We will see its power at some point in the lives of the ones we love, and some day it will come to us. It is my prayer that we will meet our Maker in a moment when we are proud of our lives, that we can look into His eyes and He will say, "Well done."

CHAPTER SEVEN

In the Dark of the Night

I WOULD NOT EVEN BEGIN TO UNDERSTAND the magnitude of my anger for Rob until long after the trial ended years later. I often wondered if he even knew the things he had put my kids through with his decision to take a gun in a moment when words or even a fist could have made his point.

Did he ever think of us? Did he know of the pain that filled my home every moment of every day? Did he wonder how I had told my children that their daddy had died? Did he really understand how many nights I have spent with paranoid children crying in my room at night asking if the man who shot their Daddy would be walking through our front door with his gun to get them? Did he ever think about the hours I've spent trying to explain why they will one day have to forgive this man... because holding on to our anger will only take us down?

He didn't hear the prayers of faith offered by a six-year-old praying about the gratitude she felt that her Dad was safe with her Father in Heaven. He didn't witness the countless prayers my babies offered for *his* children. He didn't ever see the panic attacks my babies suffered for three months every time I even stepped up off the couch to go get a drink in the kitchen... or the pain my five babies felt any time I had to go to a counseling appointment or meet with detectives. He didn't have to answer the questions... the never-ending questions: "Mommy what if someone shoots you while you are driving down the street?" or "Mommy what if you die and we have no one to take care of us?" He didn't get to walk with me and see the looks the whole town gave me. The fishbowl of love. He didn't have to wonder what the news reporters were looking for the many times they came to my door. What did they want me to say? "Oh your husband was cheating on you...and now he is dead...how does that feel?" Really?

In a moment when all I wanted was to take the time I needed to find my strength and search for peace...everyone was there watching me. But not Rob. He pulled his trigger and walked away. He didn't have to see any of it. He left me to clean up the mess that was left, and deep down, I hated him for it.

One night, I woke up to find my oldest daughter standing by my bed. It was two o'clock in the morning. She was shaking, and her voice cracked as she spoke. "Mommy, what if he is still there?" I pretended I didn't know who she was talking about. "Who, Bailey?" I asked. "The bad guy who killed Daddy? What if he is still there waiting to hurt you?" she answered. "Oh baby...I am right here. Everything is okay. We are safe." "But Mommy...I am so scared. I will never forgive him for what he did to me. I hate him Mom. I will hate him forever!" She was trembling and I could see the chills she had all over her body. How was I supposed to explain to her how to battle this fear? What was I supposed to say? How was I supposed to be a foundation for her when I myself felt a crack in my heart? How did I answer that? I had avoided even driving by the scene of the crime for fear he was there waiting for me. I knew he wasn't there, but somewhere in the back of my mind...that panic had grown strong.

I said a quick prayer to my Heavenly Father that I would know how He needed me to answer this little girl's cries. The answer came in a second. I was surrounded with peace, and my testimony of all I had ever learned about forgiveness sank deep into my heart.

We talked through the night about forgiveness and repentance and the commandment given to us to forgive all men. Everything I knew, but had forgotten, filled my soul. My words calmed my child, as the spirit calmed my mind. We talked about the Atonement and that Jesus had died on the cross for us all…even for Rob. We talked about mistakes, and that although Rob had made a really bad choice, he could have been a good man who just made the worst decision of his life. With my daughter in my arms, I felt safe in these truths. We sat in my room in the dark, surrounded by light.

There is no reboot button. Unfortunately, there is no pill to take to take away the sorrows of mortality. Like every mother's dream, I have wished I could make it all better and fix all the beliefs my children now carry inside of them about this world. I have hoped that every pain they will ever face in life could all be fixed by me.

I cannot take away their pain. I cannot heal their sorrows. I cannot protect them from all that is ugly in this world. But I can be a facilitator for my Heavenly Father who has that power. *He* is the way we find peace. *He* is the strength that can get us through anything. I have been given the words to say when I have been asked questions for which I myself needed answers. The strength in my words has not been my own. I have had a comforter of love in every way and in every moment when fear tried to destroy us. I have been blessed to be the leader of these young children as they have worked through their forgiveness and pain. And as I have watched them find peace, I too have found glimmers of light one day at a time: they have been baby-steps to find our way out of darkness.

Darkness is all around us. It can come in many forms. As we take time to seek light, we will be given strength above our own. He will carry us through the storms and help us find the rainbows at the end of the tunnel.

I know He hears our prayers. I know that even in the simple moments, He cares. Just like my love for my daughter that night, He loves each one of us. We are his sons and daughters. He cannot give us a reboot button, for we are here to learn through our struggles. But, He can and He will give us the strength to press on to a brighter day.

CHAPTER EIGHT

Where Can I Turn for Peace?

EMMETT DIED ON A FRIDAY NIGHT. SUNDAY morning came, and the last thing I needed was to go to church in my regular congregation and try to comfort anyone. I wasn't ready to hear anyone's sympathy. I didn't want to face the fact that the world found out at the same time as I, that my husband had been unfaithful. I was humiliated that I had not been enough for him. But I needed to go to church. I felt an urge. I needed to take the sacrament and feel the power that comes from it. I needed to slow down. I needed to think. I couldn't handle my own emotions, let alone take my children among a group of people trying to find peace for their own grief. I didn't want to take my kids out into the world, but I was going to go.

I asked my sister Abbey if she would come drive around with me to find a meetinghouse where we could just sneak in the back and go spend a peaceful hour listening to speakers. We didn't get too far outside of our neighborhood. In fact, we actually stopped at the first church we saw, and decided to park and go inside.

We snuck in the back and found seats. We were a few minutes late, so we had to sit in the overflow section of the chapel. It felt good to be inside the building, and I was excited to listen to any counsel that came from the talks. We sat, hand in hand. The bishop announced the program and after a hymn, it was time for the sacrament.

As the young men passed the sacrament, I just thought. I thought about my current status in life. I pondered about the years I had spent building my family. I thought about the pain that now damaged my hope. I fumbled for the words to pray...as I silently sulked in my grief.

After everyone had partaken of the bread and water, the bishop asked us to turn to another hymn. My heart skipped a beat. It was one of Emmett's and my all-time favorites, a hymn which his cousin Becky had on one of her albums that Bostyn and Bailey had loved as little girls. I would play it on repeat, over and over, on long car trips when the kids were napping, to keep them calm. It was the hymn I found Bailey singing one day when she had been put in timeout...a hymn that would be sung later that week as Emmett lay in a casket. All of these thoughts and memories began to flood my mind. The music began to play...and my tears began to fall.

Where can I turn for peace? For every wall I had built around myself, and for each stone I had tried to use to cover my pain...that hymn somehow found a way of breaking them down. Where can I turn for peace? I don't know who picked the hymn that day, but they were on an errand for *me*. The words I needed to hear more than ever before, were sung by a congregation to comfort ME, and they didn't even know I was coming that day. Each voice rang up to Heaven begging Angels to come and help me bear my grief.

Sometimes, God sends a shimmer of hope just for us. He hand-directs people to help us. I don't remember any of the words spoken that day, but the music sang to my heart. It was as if the Heavens opened up and cried..."Ashlee we are here...and we love you."

That little glimmer of hope, that tender mercy, was given to me that day because I *went* to find it. Heavenly Father *wants* to bless us. He *wants* to show us that He will orchestrate the heavens to sing for us...but first, He wants to see that we have enough faith to believe in that power. He waits outside our doors, standing with His hands open wide, but we have to be the ones to let Him in.

For every pain we have ever felt…the Savior has felt it too. We are never alone in our pain. We are never alone in our fears. We are never the only ones with sorrows. Each one of Heavenly Father's children will feel the pain of living. We cannot do it alone. That is why He sent his Only Begotten Son. The Atonement is real. He will send us the light we need if we seek Him. I would have never felt the comfort and strength that day, if I hadn't taken that first scary step to show up at that church. But I did… and He blessed me with the message I needed to hear. Heavenly messages truly are sent to comfort and strengthen us when we cannot stand, and when all we have left… is Him.

CHAPTER NINE

Grab a Gun

THE FUNERAL HAD ENDED, BUT IT DIDN'T end Teage's struggles.
In fact, he continued to get worse. He wouldn't set foot in his room, and
I had a hard time getting him to talk at all. He didn't have much of an
appetite. He had angry outbursts and kept trying to hurt me or others.
He wouldn't speak in public. The boy who used to get up smilingly to say
a prayer in church, now scratched and clawed me when I tried to get him
to leave my arms and go to his class. He didn't sleep. I didn't know what
to do. I knew he had to get some serious help, so I decided to take him
to child therapist. I had to get him to talk to someone. Anger was stirring
inside of him. I could see it all over his face.

His first counseling appointment finally came, and I was so excited to
get him there. It was like a mini-date in the car. I hadn't had much time
alone with him, and as we drove, I finally got him to talk a little bit. He
wasn't as excited about the appointment as I was, and he had many doubts
about what we were about to do. I explained to him that I would be sitting
in the room with him, and that I really needed him to be brave and share
anything that was on his mind. I encouraged him to open up and let out
any feelings he had. I told him about some of my experiences with my
counselor, and how he'd helped me talk through some of the hard things
with which I was struggling. Then I asked Teage if he had any questions.
He said, "Yeah...does this guy know any bad guys?" I wasn't sure how
to answer. I replied, "This counselor knows a lot of people, and he has

helped them with their lives. I think he is going to help us with ours."

We walked into the building. Teage held my hand so tightly, it was almost turning blue. I could feel him shaking. We sat in the waiting room, and he leaned over a few times and kissed me. He was trembling more and more, and I could tell that he was very nervous. I said, "Hey Buddy. I am so proud of you." A tear welled up in his eye and he leaned in close, "Mom, I don't want to do this." I didn't want to give him any way out, so I answered, "I know, but I'll be with you. I will be sitting right next to you, and I promise I won't leave. You can do this."

We were called into the office. I knew this counseling center well. I had started seeing a counselor here just a week before Emmett died. I had poured my heart out about all that I feared was happening in my marriage and begged the counselor to fix my "trust issues" so I could stop having so many doubts. Then, after Emmett had died, I had sat here many times trying to piece together what was left of me.

This time, however, we weren't here for me. I had come for my son. I tried hard to forget my own issues and stay focused on this little boy who was hurting so much. The counselor began talking with Teage, and I sat quietly in the corner just watching… tears silently slipping down to my neck. How did we get here? I didn't understand. How could this be my son? He was not even a child…he was only a shell of himself with glass eyes.

At first, the two of them just played. Teage would grab a dinosaur or a car and pull it through the sand. Then he would walk over to the blocks, and build something. It just seemed like a normal playroom with fun toys. I started to doubt if this was the best idea. How could running a car through the sand help bring my son back to life? Could building a tower with blocks and knocking them down really help my son find a reason to live?

Then all of the sudden, Teage grabbed a superhero and a big, green Hulk. They were just talking about normal stuff. The toy characters climbed up the couch, and then jumped off the bookshelf. Then the Hulk seemed to be getting frustrated with the superhero.

Teage looked at the therapist and said, "Sometimes bad guys get mad." The counselor said, "Oh yeah. Tell me about that." Teage replied, "Well sometimes bad guys come and hurt the good guys." "What do you mean?" the therapist asked. "Well sometimes, bad guys don't like the good guys." "Tell me about that, Teage," he encouraged. At this point Teage was slamming the Hulk into the superhero, and the superhero was not defending himself...just lying there getting body-slammed by the Hulk. Teage screamed, "Sometimes the bad guy doesn't let the good guy win."

My son threw down the little figurines, ran over to the shelf and put on a scary mask. Then he picked up a gun. It was a Nerf gun on the counter. He pointed it straight at the counselor and shot him five times in the face, emptying the gun of every Nerf bullet, then said, "And sometimes the good guy dies."

By this point, I was in the corner about to throw up...still attempting to hide my emotions and trying to figure out what the heck had just happened. My four-year-old son had clearly been playing this script in his mind for several weeks. In his view, a real-life bad guy had killed his superhero. It wasn't a movie or a video game— where the good guy came back and saved the day. Its ending was real...and it was permanent.

I thought I could handle living with the anger inside myself...but how could I bear watching my son ache to his very core? I felt like Heavenly Father kept asking me to forgive...but I kept finding reasons like this... not to forgive. It wasn't just a battle in my mind, it was a war in my heart. For every urge I had to forgive...I had a stronger urge inside of me to just let my anger consume me. For all the strength I felt I had received...this day was a big blow. I took a few steps back in my journey as I watched my son pull a trigger and shoot a man. My son wasn't afraid of losing his hat at school. He wasn't nervous that he might miss the catch in a football game at recess. He was afraid that one day, he would be the dying superhero…or even worse, the bad guy.

The night Emmett died, I made a promise to the Lord—alone in my closet—that I would forgive. I knew it would take time, but I also knew that someday, forgiveness would come. But, it sure as hell wasn't going to be that day! That day I was angry…and it felt good! When others were around, I kept my face calm on the outside…but on the inside, I was weeping tears of hate. That anger hurt unlike any pain I had ever felt… but on certain days, I actually needed that pain to keep myself moving forward.

I assume that the same type of anger I felt towards Rob, he himself felt towards Emmett. Only *I* still had a choice to make. Rob's chance to make a choice was long past. A part of me wanted Rob to hurt…as if *his* hurting would cause *my* pain to be washed away. But, in the same way that Rob's actions had not brought him peace, any pain I could have caused him to feel to bring about "justice" would not have healed me. Teage's counseling session brought me to yet another crossroad. The bitterness I felt was like a bomb waiting to be dropped…and I felt like the evil that had already wronged me once, was now trying to destroy another cherished person in my life.

The feeling of anger is real. It is strong, and it is scary. But anger is not even a concrete emotion. It is a secondhand feeling brought about by fear or some other emotion inside of us. Teage's anger at me, and everyone else around us, was not really what was driving his actions. He was sad, he was lonely, and his heart was aching. A bad guy—with two shots of a gun—had changed the way he viewed the world and his role in it.

There are so many of us walking around acting like we are angry at the universe: like somehow, everyone else owes us something, like everyone is out to get us. I know, because I have been there. Some of us show it on the outside, while others keep it inside. It is hard, when we are wronged, not to let those types of feelings consume us and gain control over who we really are. In reality, many of us are just walking around, fragmented parts of who we really can be.

What if we think of that the next time someone cuts in front of us in a line, or when someone's baby is screaming on a plane? What if the next time your son throws a fit on the floor about the outfit you chose, you really stop to listen to what is really wrong? Maybe he has been having trouble at school, or he just really misses you now that you have that new job. Would it change the way you responded? Would it help you want to show a little more love? The next time you feel that you have been taken advantage of or that someone has wronged you…stop…listen. Maybe they aren't trying to disrespect you, or offend you. Maybe they are truly just trying to cope with a pain that hurts so deeply that they don't even know where to begin to find it. Maybe each of us is just looking for answers about how to fix what feels broken in ourselves.

Watching my son that day was not something I ever expected to have to see as a mother. In fact, I never thought I would have to take one of my children to see a therapist…ever! My kids were perfect. I was striving to be the perfect parent, and they were never going to have problems. But guess what I found out? We All Have Problems! Whether it is a battle with cancer, or the death of a dog…or even just a struggle to find a real friend in our lives, we will all hurt. We will all be wronged…and we will all wrong others. We are imperfect people…and that is okay. That is why there are others out there to help us. That is what life is all about. It is about addressing our issues, owning our crap…and trying to make it right. It is learning to smile even when others are tearing us down. It is letting our pain motivate us to change ourselves. We only truly have power over our *own* existence. I believe that if we can see the world in that light…we can change the way we interact with it. We can choose the higher road and show those evils that try to take us down that we will find a way to fly.

CHAPTER TEN

Please Hold Me

KALEEYA WAS TWENTY MONTHS OLD WHEN HER daddy died. She was just a little thing. She had always been really advanced for her age—except for walking—and was wise beyond her years. We always said she had an old soul. It seemed like she knew things we didn't know, but she just hadn't quite learned how to communicate them all yet. She and Emmett had a sweet relationship. She was a bit of a daddy's girl.

My friend Kim called the day after Emmett died asking for some of his clothing. She is an amazing seamstress, and she explained to me that she wanted to make a blanket from his clothes. It was a perfect idea. I carefully went through each drawer and closet and picked only clothes that had good memories tied to them: the shirt he wore when he proposed, his favorite summer shorts he always wore at Bear Lake, and some of the kids favorite t-shirts. Every piece of clothing put into the pile to go to Kim had some sort of special memory or meaning for us.

Amazingly, Kim showed up a day later with a stack of blankets, one for me, and one for each of the kids. She shared with me how she had gone to the store to buy some fabric before she picked up the clothes. She got some odds and ends to sew together the pieces of his shirts. She had planned on making just one, big blanket. She said that as she laid it all out on her floor that night, it was as if everything just fell into place. She had exactly what she needed for six blankets, and the pieces of clothing all matched up with the pieces of fabric she had purchased. She said she had never worked so efficiently in her life, and that she was given power beyond her abilities to put together everyone's blankets.

The blankets were amazing. She laid them out in front of us and identified which blanket was for each one of us. She had felt impressed that each individual blanket was made for a specific person in our family. We sat admiring them in my living room. My brothers and sisters and parents were all sitting around when the kids came in to see their new "Daddy Blankets."

Each child was so excited to see them and instantly fell in love with his or her blanket—all the kids, that is...until I got to Kaleeya. I held up her blanket and started to explain what it was. She got an angry look on her face and ran over and punched it a few times. "Daddy?" she said. "I don't want it!" I knelt down beside her. "Kaleeya, this is a blanket made out of Daddy's clothes. Kim made this one just for you." She repeated herself, "I don't want it...Daddy gone...Mommy cries. Mommy sad. I don't want it." I tried for a few minutes to get her to see how precious this blanket would be for her, but she didn't want anything to do with it. I didn't understand. She wasn't even two years old. It didn't make sense that she would be angry at him or even understand that he was gone.

I thought back to the weeks before he died, back to the times when Emmett would get angry at me and then leave. I would go to my closet to try to calm myself down—away from the kids. While all the others would carry on playing...Kaleeya would come and find me. She would come and wipe my tears. She would ask me what was wrong. She would hold me as I cried. I never had any clue that she could understand my pain enough to be upset at Emmett. She saw me cry because of him...and now all I did was cry because he was gone. In her mind, it seems, she was mad at him for making me sad. I assumed that she had figured out that my tears were all his fault.

For a few nights, I kept trying to push the blanket on her, almost begging her to sleep with it. She always said she didn't want it and added,

"Mommy cries." Each night was the same. I would tell her how special it was, and she would push it away.

After putting the kids to bed one night I went downstairs. I was sitting on the couch and within a few minutes, I heard quiet sobbing. I wasn't sure which room it was coming from so I tiptoed up the stairs and listened quietly at each door. At Kaleeya's door, I discovered that she was the source of those tears. I opened her door and walked in the room towards her. I couldn't see her face until I got closer. She was reaching her arms out and sobbing, "Daddy... I sorry. Hold me Daddy. Hold me Daddy. I sorry Daddy... I happy now... Please come back... I hold you... I need you hold me, Daddy."

I looked in the direction that her hands were extended, and there on her dresser was a picture of her and Emmett. It was an oversized photo that my friend Gaby had blown up for the funeral. I picked up the picture and grabbed her Daddy Blanket from the side of her crib, then I scooped her up and sat down with all three on my lap. For the first time, I noticed that the shirt he was wearing in the picture was the same piece of clothing that was sewn into her Daddy Blanket.

She was still sobbing to the picture. "Daddy died. He gone." I said, "I know baby. I am so sorry. Mommy is here." "My daddy in heaven and I want him to hold me, Mommy. I need him to come and hold me." Now she was almost begging the picture to come to life. With a lump in my throat, I told her how much her daddy loved her, but that he wasn't here and he wasn't going to be coming back. Then I held up the Daddy Blanket. "Daddy isn't going to hold you tonight, but your Daddy Blanket was sewn by Angels so he can be wrapped all around you." I wrapped my baby girl in her daddy's clothes, and rocked her. We rocked and we cried together, wishing we could understand why a blanket was all that was left of the smile that stared back at us from the photograph.

Our little ones are holding their hands out to us... begging for us to hold them and to see them as the precious little jewels they are. All

around us, people are reaching out for something. Waiting to be forgiven. Waiting to feel love. Our wives are silently waiting for us to look them in the eyes and tell them they are enough. Our husbands need to hear how grateful we are for them. In one way or another, we are holding our hands out for someone to hear our cries...waiting to feel complete from the love we need someone else to show us. But sometimes, those words and that love we seek, is not ever going to come. Whether from death, or pure selfishness, we may never hear or feel that love we need so desperately.

I wasn't what Kaleeya wanted that night, but I got to give her what she needed. She needed to feel like she was safe and important to him. She craved to feel the love she had lost. I was a poor replacement for the man she needed to hold her, but Heavenly Father sent me in his place. Emmett wasn't ever going to come back to fill that void...but that night, I was lucky enough to have the chance to try.

As you look around...watch for the hands reaching out for you. Put down your phones and enjoy the pure excitement of sliding down the slide at the park. Put your computers away and build a block tower... just so you can hear them giggle when they knock it over. Next time your

husband walks in that door…throw your arms around him and let him know how grateful you are for all that he *does* do for you. When your woman walks in asking if her outfit looks ugly…let her know how stunning she is. Look into the eyes of everyone who speaks to you…and less into the screens that consume your thoughts. Search for the hearts that need your time. Seek for the souls who are literally begging for someone to notice them. Like our Savior, find the one who is lost…and lead that person back to where he or she feels safe and loved.

We are all reaching out for someone to hold us. Every human on earth has a basic need to be loved. In those dark days when you have spent all night crying and reaching…and you feel like no one has heard your pleas…remember that Heavenly Father is there. Sometimes, we have to find our feelings of worth through only ourselves and God. Reach your hands out to him. Extend your arms toward Heaven and seek the light from God. Ask Him to shed His love upon you, to help you see your own worth. He loves you. He wants to wrap you up in His love and rock you while you cry. Let Him. Ask Him to send you His Angels. And then when they come…let them sing you the lullabies you aren't hearing anywhere else. Let their songs whisper to your heart.

You are not alone. They are closer than you know.

CHAPTER ELEVEN

Not About You

I THINK IN MY CLOSET THE NIGHT of Emmett's death... I naively believed Heavenly Father's sweet reassurance that I could handle it, somehow meant that it was going to be easy, and that every day I would be strong. I thought that from that point forward, all would be simple and smooth, and that every new angle of the tasks I had ahead of me would come with little or no care. I had been through the hard stuff already, right? I felt that because of all we had already suffered, our ticket to peace and healing should have been a free ride. I wish I would have realized then that I still had many battles to fight... and many doubts to come. Living in denial became my life-support. In denial... I wasn't a widow. I wasn't left to take care of my children without a partner. Emmett hadn't really been shot in the head and in the heart. Denial was my strength. Every breath seemed easier when I could pretend it wasn't real.

Then on other days, despair paralyzed me with its power. I was not available for my kids in the way I wanted to be. There are complete twenty-four-hour periods for which I still have no clue what they ate, who got them dressed, or if Tytus and Kaleeya got their naps. Some days, I was kept busy away from them dealing with the paperwork involved in a death and the grim realities of a murder investigation. On other days, I was busy inside my own head, trying to figure out how to be a person and a mother again. Both of those types of days were scary for me. I had moments where I could see their love... but couldn't feel it. I felt frozen and trapped in my own body.

I had never really understood commercials about depression medication when they stated that "all the things that used to bring you joy now feel dull and impossible" until now. I had a few days when even my kids were just reminders of the lies that had destroyed my marriage. Everything that had once brought me joy—like cooking and cleaning, and teaching my children—was now a monumental task that only reminded me of the life I had lost.

I felt guilty when I was away from my children, but I had no choice. The times when I *was* with them—and my mind was lost someplace else—are the days I wish I could get back. I had so many wonderful people who picked up the slack to allow those days to pass. Random neighbors, family members, and friends seemed to show up just at the very moment I needed them. My kids were always looked after, meals were always warm, and everyone always knew they were loved. At those times when I wasn't able to be the mother I wanted to be, someone was always there to pick up the slack. For those miracles, I will forever be grateful.

One of those days stands out clearly in my mind. It was the day on which I had an afternoon appointment with detectives at Emmett's office to sign over his computers and both his and Kandi's cell phones as evidence in the murder investigation. I felt sick to my stomach all day. It was the kind of uneasy feeling that makes you so nauseous you can't even take a bite of food...you have to force-feed yourself. And the nervous body shakes were like constant tremors in my limbs. I think my body had been in a state of perpetual nervousness for a long time. It was how I felt any time I had to go down to Emmett's office to deal with business stuff, and it was always worse when I had to meet with the detectives. The brutality of his murder was more difficult for me to wrap my brain around than his death, or even the affair.

So this particular morning, I was mentally absent. I was surrounded by fog and my zombie mode was in full force. My phone began to ring...

and it didn't stop for several hours. Some posts made on Facebook had detectives and family members, as well as some of Emmett's former co-workers, up in arms. There had been threats and accusations made that were not going over well.

Originally after Emmett died, I kept his Facebook page up to serve as a memorial stop for anyone who wanted to share a kind thought or memory of him. However, I quickly began to question the wisdom of that idea when comments made by other women implied that they had spent time with my husband just days before his death. I tried a few times to get into his account in hopes of editing out some of the unflattering comments made by those women, as well as other questionable comments posted by friends I didn't know, but my attempts failed. I had tried every single password we had ever used. Nothing worked, and so I stopped trying. My ego was severely damaged, but I figured I had no other choice than to live with it. I couldn't take back those comments on Facebook any easier than I could change the fact that the stories being told were actually true.

So that day, after I got off the phone with several frustrated callers, I tried even harder to crack the code. I made up every kind of password I could think of. I was in tears…mainly about the comments I wanted deleted, and less about the threats against Rob, and Emmett's former employees and employers for all they should have known. I sat at my computer for hours trying to get a hold of anyone who could help me figure out the password, and like a compulsive dog with a bone, typing in imaginary passwords over and over and over.

Finally, the time came for me to leave if I was going to make it downtown in time to meet with everyone. I went into my bedroom to change my clothes and fix my mess of a face. As I washed the mascara off my cheeks, I stared at myself in the mirror. "Ashlee," I thought, "why are you making this about you? This isn't about your pride. This isn't about what others think about you…or about Emmett, for that matter. This is about a group of people who are all hurting each other. They are blaming each other. They are threatening. You need to think about them. You need to worry about your children's future and safety. You need to find answers to this for them, NOT FOR YOU!"

That was it. For the past six hours, I had been going about it all wrong. I had been so consumed by my own pride that I wasn't doing any of this for anyone but me. I knelt down beside my bed and began to change the way I asked for help. I prayed that I could find a way to fix what had been going on that day...that I could find someone—or something—to help me stop all of the horrible comments from being posted. I begged that, whatever it took, I could keep my babies safe from such hurtful words in the future...and from anyone whose actions could hurt them now."

I stood up and grabbed my purse and keys. I walked towards the door into the garage. As I reached for the handle, a jumbled mix of words and numbers came to my mind. I stood there gripping the doorknob, not quite understanding what any of it meant. Then like a light bulb going on, I knew it was the password.

I dropped my purse and ran back to my computer. Within one minute, Emmett's Facebook page was totally shut down. All of the hateful words spoken...gone. All of the threats and accusations...erased. All of the embarrassing memories...deleted.

I wasn't available for my kids that day. I have no idea if I told them I loved them or not. I don't even know if I kissed them goodbye. But I was able to do *something* for them. Once I let go of my pride and stopped thinking about myself, I was given the inspiration I needed to keep them safe. That password certainly didn't come to my mind because of anything I was doing correctly as a mother at that time. It came as a protection for *other* people who needed to feel safe. It came to me because Heavenly Father loved my children and wanted to give me the power to protect them. My ego wasn't important to Him. When I let go of myself, I was given the answers to my prayers.

It is easy to put yourself first. It is natural. It feels safe. It is a fight or flight mechanism with which we are all innately born. "What is in it for me? What do I get out of this relationship or deal? If I do something nice for someone else…am I doing it to see them succeed and find happiness…or do I have my own back in mind?" When we are focused on ourselves, we do not truly see anyone else. We are blinded by our own power and pride. The world is for us to use…at any cost.

That belief is untrue! It is a lie that destroys relationships and families. It is a powerful force that can rip apart all that is good. Darkness in your heart will lead you to serve yourself…and eventually, all you will have left…is yourself. One feel-good-in-the-moment selfish decision after another in life will bring you to live life all alone. Even the power of darkness that pulls you away from the ones you love will, in the end, eventually leave you. Satan makes no permanent friends. He doesn't wait around to see how you cope.

True joy comes when we put others ahead of ourselves, when we allow God to steer our course. I know that every day can seem a little bit more daunting than the last. The moments we stand can, at times, seem impossible. But true joy will not come if all we have is ourselves. Take care of the people who stand in those moments with you. Even if you can't feel the love that is pouring out all over you…when the darkness fades, eventually you will be able to find it and focus on it. That love will be stronger than any selfish desire that tried to take you away from it.

Sometimes, there is a quiet whispering that speaks to our souls. It is a voice that helps us when we need to feel comforted. It is a peace that holds us when we need to feel loved. It is a calm that reassures us that it is all going to be okay. I was blessed that afternoon with a quiet whisper. It was a miraculous moment for me. I know that miracles are real. I know that even when we feel we don't deserve it, we are still given reassurance that even in the small things…God cares about US.

CHAPTER TWELVE

Alone

WELL, IT CAME. THE DAY WHEN EVERYONE returned back to their normal lives. I hadn't realized that the world was still turning. I wasn't ready, not even a little bit. I knew this was the night I would put my kids to bed, and I would go to bed, alone. My mother had to go back home. Everyone had to get back to their own lives...back to the normal they had always known.

My neighbor Auna was like a second mother to me through everything. Just weeks before Emmett died, I had shared with her my fears about what was going on with him. And then when he died, I texted her just hours after I found out about what had happened. She was nine-months pregnant, but she came over in the middle of her sleep. She made food for everyone who was already gathering. She sat and rubbed my feet. And every day since Emmett's death, she had checked on me.

Now on this day, she said she would be coming over to get me off the couch and work out with me. As soon as my kids were in bed, she was at the door, ready to break a sweat. I didn't feel at all like working out, but I did appreciate the thought that she could help me get through some of the hours I would be spending alone in the silence.

We started our workout. Auna turned on the TV and noticed that I had a few episodes of the television comedy *The Office* that were recorded, and hadn't been watched. She selected the first recorded episode.

The minute the theme music from the show began, my mind went back four years to the first time Emmett and I had watched *The Office*. Teage was just a few days old, and my stepbrother Grant and his wife Heather had loaned us a copy of the show's first season. While trying to get Teage to sleep in the early evening hours, we would turn on an episode and laugh and laugh. We had found a new favorite show.

At every family get-together, and every other chance we got, we tried to "sell" the show to everyone we knew. They just had to become as obsessed as we were with the best show ever! We exchanged *The Office* souvenirs with my siblings for Christmas. I even did a Dundee Awards ceremony one year with actual "Dundees" I made from bowling trophies from *Deseret Industries*, our goodwill store. *The Office* was *our* show, and we never missed it.

Every note of that opening theme-song was like a flashback of the hours Emmett and I had spent sharing the show. I couldn't enjoy it without him there. I didn't know how to watch it without him. I didn't want to watch it if he wasn't with me.

My heart hurt. I wasn't sure how it could be, but somewhere under all of my pain and anger towards Emmett... I still missed him. My chest got tighter and tighter as we did our workout while watching the episode. We must have talked a little bit afterwards, but all I remember is walking her to the door. As the door shut and I turned the lock, every good memory I had of Emmett surrounded me.

I ran to my room. It was quiet. It was empty and cold. I was alone in that room. Nobody was there to pick up the slack that night. I was the only person my children would wake up to when the clock hit seven a.m. the next morning. I fell to the floor, and it jolted me when my face smacked the carpet. It was a physical reminder that all of this was real, and I despised it. This wasn't a movie. It hadn't been a dream. The carpet smelled clean. It was soft on my cheek. I couldn't move.

My heart ached for the man I had married. I yearned to hear his voice. I thought about calling his cell phone just to hear his voice ask the caller to leave a message. Then I remembered the detectives had his phone.

I lay face down on my floor... waiting for someone to come pick me up. I cried for all the years that had slipped away. I wept for the man to whom I had given my life. I screamed for the fact that no one was there to hear my anguished cries. I didn't understand. I was so mad at the man who had taken something so sacred and shared it with another woman, but I still longed to be held by that same man who had shared it with me.

I thought about the day Emmett and I first met. I was just a young twenty-year-old working at the workout facility at Utah State University. From the first moment we met, I knew this man was different. The first time we kissed, I felt safe in his arms. We had everything going for us. We knew exactly what we wanted, and we were both bullheaded enough to accomplish our wildest dreams. And we had the same dreams. Through the coming

years, we watched those dreams come true... one after another.

I remembered the day we got married. We were so excited. We couldn't wait to be together in the temple. We planned it all. It was exactly how I always thought it would be. It was an amazing day, and we felt a bright future just waiting before us.

I pictured the day Emmett proposed to me. He had the ring in his pocket when he took me to a bridge overlooking the place where his childhood home used to sit. Now, it was just a beautiful field with a stream and a bridge. The bridge was covered with snow. It was freezing that night, but I was so excited, I didn't care. He got down on one knee and told me all the reasons why he wanted to spend the rest of his life with me. He promised that he would give me the best of everything. He assured me that I would always be the woman of his dreams.

I pictured every Christmas we had shared. All the New Year's holidays we had spent with our good friends Emily and Evan. I thought about every birthday. Every Easter dress Emmett had picked out for our girls. Every Valentines Day card he had ever written.

I pictured driving to the Oregon Coast on our honeymoon. It was a perfect week. I thought about all the choices I had made to keep myself

pure. I had saved myself in every way for him.

I thought about the birth of each of our children. The hours he spent holding my hand. All of our babies had picked *us* to be their parents. They were all so unique, and yet they were right where they belonged. Each child brought something new and exciting and completed us as a family even more.

I thought about watching Emmett on his skis doing flips off a ramp the first weekend he took me to Bear Lake to meet his cousins. He was such a show-off, but he was so talented in everything he did. It was so adorable the way he looked at me to see if I was watching. And I was... I didn't want to miss anything he did, and I wanted to be a part of it. I loved being his partner and feeling like we could conquer the world. That is all

I had ever wanted: to love and be loved in return. I thought about all the years I actually lived that dream.

But now, here I was...face down on my bedroom floor...ALONE.

Memories. That was all I had left. I wanted to text him to remind him of all the things that had made us so special. Remind him of the moments we had shared together...but he wasn't there. On that night, reality hit me like a rock. The man I had loved was gone, and for the first time since his death, I truly allowed myself to miss him. No one was watching. Nobody was there to see. Just me. All alone, missing his love. Missing his laugh. Missing the funny things he said. Missing the moments we stood together. Missing everything about him.

I knew he wasn't a perfect man when I married him, but I loved him anyway. He wasn't always the perfect husband, but he was *my* husband. Even in those months before he was gone, when I knew something was wrong, I never stopped loving him.

The pain in my heart didn't allow me to get off the floor that night, but the love in my memories filled a little bit of the hole that was left in it. But that didn't change the fact that I was still ... alone.

CHAPTER THIRTEEN

Last Words

I REMEMBER A DAY SITTING AT THE play land at McDonald's. I am not sure if anyone else was there, but my kids were just running around having fun. Tytus was in my arms. Tears were falling down my face. I watched the kids as they played, but my mind was elsewhere. It had gone back in time...rehearsing over and over the day Emmett died.

Friday, March 11, 2011. I spent the whole day preparing to spend a wonderful evening together as a family. I had made all of Emmett's favorite foods. The kids were dressed to the nines. I had decided no one would go to sleep that night until we spent some quality time together as a family. I needed Emmett to see that these babies and I knew he was at a low point...but that we still loved him with all of our hearts. Everything was just waiting for him. A few hours went by, but he still wasn't home. I had my mind made up...we would all be waiting for him when he got home. We waited...and waited.

Finally, I heard the garage door open, and his truck pulled in. Emmett walked into the house. He was expressionless. He didn't notice any of my preparations. I tried to give him a kiss, but he just threw his head to the side and walked towards the kitchen. I asked about his day. No reply. He just kept looking out the window and checking his phone. The baby was asleep in his bouncy chair and the kids had gone off to play upstairs, so I decided this might be an opportunity for me to speak alone with him. I followed Emmett into the kitchen and hoisted myself up onto the countertop next to him.

We chit-chatted for a minute. As we sat there in the kitchen, he said, "I can't wait to go to a counselor one of these days so he can tell you how crazy you are!" My heart dropped. This was not the conversation I had been looking forward to having.

I said, "So that is our answer? We just need a counselor to tell us how crazy I am…and that will fix our marriage? You honestly don't think you play any role in what has been going on in this house the last few months?" For the first time in weeks, I had dared to question out loud something he had said.

He stared back at me, shocked. "What the hell would he tell *me* to do better?" I said, "Do you…do you…really want me to tell you?" Emmett replied, "Yeah, Ash, tell me what on earth a counselor would ever say to *me*!" So I said, "Well…will you listen and let me talk? Will you let me share some things I've been struggling with…without getting mad at me?" He said, "I won't say a word!"

So, I began…"Well I think he might touch on the subject of the kids missing you and wanting you to be a part of their lives…" He sat silently. I continued, "And I've felt you have pushed me away, especially in an area that used to be such a healthy part of our marriage. I feel like when you don't want to be intimate or even sleep in the same room as me, that either I'm not doing it for you…" I couldn't breathe… "or that someone else is!" He lost it. He began screaming at the top of his lungs. Still to this day, I know Angels must have held earmuffs over my children's ears, because they didn't hear a thing. I could barely hear their laughter upstairs over his screams. I *had* to get through to him.

I grabbed his face with both my hands and said, "I need you to listen to me right now. I love you. I have always loved you. I am not going anywhere. I know something is going on with you. I need you to talk to me and quit pushing me away. I miss you. Whatever it is…I am prepared to support you through it. I have been to the temple, I have talked to a counselor... I know we can do this. I have been asking my family to pray for us. They believe in us. We all believe in you, Emmett. I am willing and wanting to know what role I have played in harming our relationship, and I want to be better for you. These kids and I are not going anywhere... but I need you to trust me right now when I tell you that I can't take much more of this... without knowing that we are all on the same team and that we are working together to finding answers for our family."

He stopped shaking and for just a few seconds, there was a glimmer of the old Emmett in his eyes. He took a few long breaths and said, "Ash... I am scared... I don't know what I am doing... please be patient and wait for me... I am so scared." Just then, his phone beeped with a new text message. As if a magician had waved his wand... Emmett snapped out of his moment of sincerity. Then he threw my hands off his face, and at the top of his lungs, he screamed "You and your f...ing family can just go to Hell... You guys don't care about me. You hate me! You don't love me... I could kick all their asses..." He yelled out threats against my brothers and the rest of us, and then screamed that he didn't want or need any of us.

In a worked up frenzy, he ran into our bedroom, yelling at me as he left the kitchen. I was shaking, and tears were streaming down my face. I fell to the kitchen floor, not sure about what to do next. A few minutes later, the kids came downstairs. I picked myself up off the floor and tried to put on my happy smile. I sat them down around the table and began to serve them all of Emmett's favorite foods, now a very cold dinner. As they began to take bites, Emmett came and took his seat at the head of the table, as he had hundreds of times at any normal family dinner.

I began to dish up his food, but he said, "I am not going to eat this crap." He just sat with a blank gaze... and watched the kids eat his favorite dinner. When they were done, he told them all to go to the couch to watch TV with him. He leaned over to me and said, "See, I am a good dad..."

They had only been watching TV for a few minutes when Emmett's phone rang. He answered and addressed the caller by name. It was the close family friend I had e-mailed, begging him to check up on Emmett sometime that week. I had shared with him some of my concerns about our marriage. He was not only one of Emmett's best friends, but he was also a family therapist—someone I hoped could shed some light on what to do…if only Emmett would open up to him.

Emmett stepped into our bedroom to continue his conversation. The baby monitor was on in our bedroom, so I could hear his voice coming from the receiver in the kitchen. At first, I walked over to turn it down to give him some privacy, but then I decided I had better take this opportunity to hear just what he had to say about the problems in our marriage. At first, I could only hear bits and pieces of the conversation because the kids were playing nearby. Since it was already way past their bedtime, I decided to get them all tucked into bed and not worry too much about the conversation going on in our bedroom.

Once the kids were in bed, I went back to the kitchen and took a seat next to the monitor to see if I could pick up any tips as to how to start the process to heal our home. What I heard was devastating. Not a single word I heard Emmett speak about me was true. I knew I had shortcomings as a wife: faults, insecurities and fears. I also had shortcomings as a parent…and in all aspects of my life, for that matter, but the things I heard being said about me were out and out lies.

I felt the same way I had felt a few days earlier, when I had walked out of the counselor's office. The information I heard that night gave me no direction and still left me with no answers as to how to be there for my husband, or what to change in myself to be a better wife to him. When their conversation was over, he walked out of the room with a big grin on his face. "Well, he thinks you are as crazy as I do, so I guess this IS all your fault. He said that you make him sick, and he believes every word I told him about you."

I sighed, my heart pounding out of my chest. "Well, what about me, Em? Don't I get a chance to talk to him?" He muttered, "Do whatever you want...but you aren't touching my phone." So I grabbed my own phone and headed to our bedroom. I felt a need to share the feelings and fears that had been plaguing me for the past few months. I got him on the phone and began to pour it all out. ... He was definitely prepared to tell me I was crazy. Emmett was an excellent attorney, and with his well-crafted arguments, he had made certain that his friend wouldn't listen to a thing I had to say.

In the middle of our conversation, Emmett walked into the room and said, "I'm going to Walgreens to grab some medicine." I held the phone away from my ear and begged, "Please, just wait, please...we can talk about what you guys talked about. Let's just spend the night together and try to figure this out....Please stay! Emmett, I am begging you. I need you to stay here!" He shot back, "No...don't tell me what to do! I'm going to go."

And those were the last words he would ever say to me. I would never hear his voice again. Those were the words that would ring in my ears for-ever. They would ring in my soul, and they didn't just speak to me in *that* moment. They said to me over and over again, "You aren't worth staying for, you aren't worth my time. You aren't pretty enough, you aren't skinny enough. You're not worth living for or fighting for." Every doubt I had ever had in my life... now rang out in my ears. Those doubts rang true and they rang out clearly. I *wasn't* good enough. I *wasn't* worth fighting for, and no one in his right mind would ever see that I *was* good enough. I felt like I would always be just a broken piece of the "me" I had once been.

As I played out the scene of that horrible evening over and over again as I sat there in McDonalds, I could feel myself getting smaller and small-er. I could smell the fries and chicken nuggets...My kids were all around me. I could hear the orders being placed...people were everywhere. The world was spinning around me...nobody was standing still. My children would come up and give me kisses every few minutes. I could see their cute smiles. I could hear their soft giggles as they went up and down the slide...but all I could FEEL was the despair that this truth left inside of me. I WAS nothing.

Why hadn't I been enough that night? What could I have done or said to make him want to stay? That day at McDonald's wasn't the first time, and it wouldn't be the last, when my body stood in the moment...but my mind was somewhere stuck in the past, frozen in anguish.

You cannot rewrite the past...not even with all the hurt and anger of the world. My fears all came true in one night, and now they were screaming inside of me...that I was worth NOTHING. That I was not even worth living for...and that I wasn't even the one he died fighting for.

Emmett knew I wasn't going to give up on him...but he was also so afraid of losing us that he thought it would be easier to let his secrets destroy him...inside. I have never been in that situation. I can only imagine that after one lie turns into another, it is just easier to push everyone away, and pretend that everything is someone else's fault.

What if he had just let us in? What if he had told me everything that night? Maybe it wouldn't have changed the outcome of the following hours, but it would have changed some things for *me*. I'm sure he thought he'd have all the chances in the world to come back and apologize for the secrets he was keeping from us, the lies he was trying so hard to conceal. I know his words and actions that evening aren't what he would have wanted our last memories of him to be. It hurts deep in my soul...for him...that they are.

We will all speak our last words one day. Just as true as the sun will rise, we will all have a morning that will be the final time we walk out our front door...never to return. What will your last words be? What 'I am sorry' will be left unsaid? If you were to die today, what will echo in the hearts and minds of those you love? What memories will your family be left with...if this breath you take right now...were to be your final breath?

For everyone who walks the earth...now is your time. Now is OUR time to decide how we want to be remembered when we leave this mortal world. Now is the moment to speak our last words...every single day.

Now is our time to stand in the places in which we find ourselves, and to love with all of our hearts.

Make every moment count. Take every opportunity to make your last words the ones that truly come from the heart. Leave every room better than when you entered it...before you turn around and shut that door. Smile as you leave, just in case that image is the last one your loved ones will have left...of the "you" they will remember.

I have watched myself feel small. I have believed with all of my heart that I was worthless. I have had regrets about things I said and things I heard. I have felt the despair of words left unsaid...but one thing I have come to understand is that the past doesn't determine our future. We *don't* have to be what we once were. We are *not* always destined to fall. Even if we have wronged everyone we have ever known, it is never too late to change the words we say or the script we are writing. We have the power to decide who we want to be and what we will become. We can't change the past...but we can help write the future.

Now is the time to live with your last words on your lips, so that when the time comes, you can leave everything behind with no regrets. Live those moments that will never be forgotten as the person Christ would want you to be.

CHAPTER FOURTEEN

A Dream of Hope

TO TRULY FORGIVE, WE MUST LET GO of all feelings of contention
and no longer harbor ill feelings towards someone we feel has wronged us.
To repent, we must not only right our wrongs with the people whom we
have hurt, but we must also make right with God those things for which we
are asking to be forgiven. Forgiveness and repentance were two words I had
heard a million times in my life. I had even studied them in depth in books
and in scripture. But until I had to apply them in context, for myself, I had
no idea of the impact and power of their weight on my soul.

At the beginning of this tragedy, I thought forgiveness of all parties
involved would merely come as a moment when I could check the "forgiveness" category off a list ... and all would feel right again. I even walked
around for a long time pretending in my mind, that I *had* forgiven each
of them, and that it would never be a serious issue for me. I didn't know
how wrong I was. Each day since that horrible event has been a step in the
process of forgiveness and a series of moments that have taught me how
to apply the Atonement of Jesus Christ in my life.

I not only faced the pain of having to forgive, but I had also allowed
darkness to creep inside of me, for which I had to truly repent. Furthermore, I had regrets for things I wish I had done ... and should have done before the tragedy. Moments when I should have been more brave and acted
on the fears inspiring me to dig deeper to find answers. Instead of following
those promptings, I allowed my emotions and insecurities to keep me from

bringing to light the things that could have helped my family.

I had so many moments that played over and over in my mind...so many regrets of things left unsaid, and worse, moments when I should have just shut my big fat mouth and not said some of the things I said out of fear. Just as Emmett hadn't always been the perfect husband...I hadn't always done the right thing, or said the right things as his wife. That truth was hard to face, especially after he was gone.

There were many wasted days I spent racking my brain about how I could have done things differently. And many lonely nights filled with tears, begging Heavenly Father to forgive me for my imperfections in my marriage. Though I have come to feel peace with the truth that his death didn't happen because of me, and that his choosing to have an affair was not my fault or a reaction to anything I did or did not do, it has nonetheless been hard not to put the blame on myself and my imperfections as his wife...whether real or imagined.

Forgiving a man who would never be able to ask for my forgiveness was like living in a room with no windows...but being asked to use the light of the moon to see. I had put my entire energy into finding harmony in our marriage, and now that I was only left with myself...all I could do was make ME whole again.

I tossed and turned, knowing that forgiveness would have to come for me in a form that I had never before experienced. Forgiveness, to me, had always meant that you say you are sorry, they say they are sorry, and you forgive each other and move on. Now it was just me. Nobody lying next to me in my bed to lean over and tell me how sorry he was for the mess he had left me to clean up and all the pain he had caused me. He wasn't even there to tell *me* how *I* could have been a better person...or wife for him.

So, one night after everyone had gone back to their own lives...as I lay in bed alone, I prayed for a shimmer of hope...a moment or a means to find the peace I needed to forgive him.

That night I had a dream. All around me were piles of something white.

As I got closer to them, I could see that they were all letters. They went on for miles and miles, like the ocean. I just stared at them unaware of why they were all there. As I reached out my hand to pick up one of them...all of the sudden Emmett was standing next to me. His eyes looked somber. He had a tear trickling down his face. He leaned in and spoke into my ear. He said, "They are all from me, Ash....It is everything I should have said, everything I didn't say, and everything I am sorry for." I stood frozen, staring at him, not knowing what to say. I looked out at all the letters. They looked as though they went on forever, and they stacked up higher than a building. I couldn't even see an end. I turned back towards him to ask him all of the questions that had been weighing on me...but he was gone.

Why would he leave? Couldn't he just stay and read them to me? My eyes searched for him up and down the mountains of envelopes...but the more I searched the horizon, the more I realized he wasn't there. I began to panic. Why would he just say those few words and then abandon me again? Didn't he know I needed him to answer so many of my questions? Didn't I deserve just a few more minutes of his time? I stood there for a long time, trying to figure out why he had left. Eventually, my heart stopped racing and I calmed myself down and decided to just start reading.

I picked up the first letter. I slowly tore open the envelope...."My Dearest Ashlee, I am sorry that you are alone. I am sorry that I am gone. You have no idea how much I wish I was there with you." Next letter....I opened it a little faster, craving to read his next words. "I am sorry I wasn't there for you when you needed me the most." By now, I was racing to open each letter, "I wish I would have known that my choices would have caused us so much pain...I didn't mean to hurt you." "I am sorry you are doing it all by yourself." Next. "I should have been true to you. You deserved my whole heart...but I didn't save it for you." "I miss you." "Please don't let your fear of our past keep you from living your life." "Please let yourself move forward with faith." "I wish I would have cherished my family." "I wish I would have come home a little earlier every night." "I wish you could feel the regret I have so you could see how much I am hurting for the things I put you through." "I wish I would have laughed more." "Please help our kids remember the 'me' you fell in love with." "Please help others who are where *I* was in life so they can learn from my mistakes." "I am sorry I lied." "I am sorry I abandoned all the truth that I once knew." "I am sorry I didn't just tell you everything and make it right." "I wish I had known that was my last Christmas...I would have spent more time with you." "I wish I would have been more engaged when Tytus was born, that I wouldn't have kept texting and leaving you alone in the hospital." "I wish I could see Tytus take his first steps, Teage play football, the twins have their first date, Kaleeya play with her Doggy Doggy." "I wish I hadn't gone on that trip before I died." "I am sorry I involved Teage in my lies...the way he is suffering now is not only because I am gone, it is because of what I did." "Please tell my story to others so no one else has to feel the anguish that is torturing me." "I am sorry you feel worthless...I wish I would have showed you how priceless you are to me." "I wish I would have made more promises and never broken them." "I wish I could hold you and take away your pain." "Ashlee, please help the kids be strong. They need you. You are all they have now." "Please live a life you will be proud of." "Please know that I love you." "I wish I could do it all over again. I would have put you all first."

Mountains of words I needed to hear—all night long. I climbed the peaks of letters and soaked in every phrase. All the things I was begging to hear the night he died, all the things I wish he would have said. Though I still will never actually hear the words from his mouth, that dream has brought me so much peace. It has been a pillar of love in the healing and forgiving process, which has been required for my journey. I know it was just a dream, but at that point in my healing, for me it was a powerful vision.

We all have mountains to climb. Sometimes we have to climb to the highest peaks before we can find the answers to our prayers. I have felt the mountains of regret...but that night, I was blessed to reach a summit of words filled with peace. Each letter was like a weight being lifted off of me.

I had been wronged on so many levels. I had craters of pain that ran deep inside of my soul. But I loved Emmett and I loved my Heavenly Father for carrying me when I could not stand. I had to let it go and carry on. That I knew now without a doubt.

I had to be strong for my little children, who would soon be going back to school and facing the world. They were going to have their own journeys in life. Emmett wouldn't be able to see any of it, as part of our family here on earth. I had to figure out how to put one foot in front of the other... and carry on, and I felt grateful to be the one here with them through it all.

Forgiveness is not easy, yet it is required of us to forgive all men. My internal checklist of forgiveness did not end that night, just like it didn't end on my knees in my closet when Emmett died. These were merely the first steps in a series of bleachers I had yet to climb. My heart and soul still had miles to run before they would catch up... but it was a sweet, tender mercy to read the words I had been longing to hear.

Heavenly Father knows that sometimes our pinnacles are greater than we can handle alone. That is why he sent us a Savior. I didn't have to carry around this pain. It was not mine to bear all by myself. There will always be a burden around each of our necks in one way or another. There will always be another hill to climb before we can reach the peace at the end of the road. Our journeys can sometimes feel unbearable. We might feel like we have been abandoned, overlooked, or that we are insignificant or alone. We are never alone.

I know that every word in those letters was not just a gift from Emmett, it was a blessing from my Heavenly Father, who knew exactly what I was feeling. *He* had been there before I was, and now He was there for ME. I know He had been watching me and wishing He could take away my pain. He cannot take away our pain... but He will give us little glimmers of His love. He will send us blessings in those moments that will be the most valuable for us.

For me, my hope came in envelopes stamped with love from all the Heavenly beings who were cheering me on, and I knew now, that even Emmett believed in me. That dream was the beginning of a journey that I now knew I wasn't taking alone.

CHAPTER FIFTEEN

On Sacred Ground

THE TWINS KEPT BEGGING TO GO BACK to school. I think they craved the feeling of the "normal life" they had known when they were there. The desire to let them go rustled in me...and yet, I was not ready to send them off, out of my care. I knew eventually that day would come, but I resisted, and put it off for as long as I could. I even considered home schooling...but I knew I was in no state to be the sole provider for my children's education. The day inevitably came. As the car got closer to the school, my thoughts turned back...to the last time I had spoken with their teacher...

It was exactly one week before Emmett died. I found a note in both of my daughters' backpacks informing us that they had been in a fight at school and had been sent to the office. My twins? The calmest, 'chillest,' most easy-going little kindergartners anyone had ever seen? Those girls had gotten into a fight? I needed to hear the details.

So the next day, I loaded my three youngest ones into the car and headed over to the school to pick up the girls. I parked right in front of their classroom door so I could leave the babies in the car while I went to talk to their teacher about the events that had taken place the day before. I walked up to her and gestured for her to come speak to me privately, away from all the kids who surrounded her. I asked her what had happened.

She recounted the story of the fight, informing me that a boy had 'messed' with Bailey, and Bostyn had just taken him out! She literally threw him to the ground, and he hit his head on the concrete. Then another boy came over, trying to get in the middle of it, and *Bailey* punched *him* in the stomach. I just looked at the teacher in amazement, like she was full of crap…my mouth wide open.

My twins, the little girls who never even fought with each other had taken on some older boys? I explained to her that I was grateful for her patience with them, and then burst into tears. "We have some stuff going on at our house right now…I am trying to figure it all out.…Please just know that my girls are trying their best…and I just need you to please be patient with them. This outburst of anger is not entirely their fault."

Now she was staring at me like *I* was making up stories. She put her arm around me and said, "If you need to talk to someone, the school counselor is always available to help." I realized I had better stop making a scene, and I started to wipe my tears. "Thanks for listening…sorry, I don't know why I am crying, I just…I just don't know what is going on…and I don't know how to make it all okay for them."

I took the twins to the car, buckled them in their car seats and pulled away from the classroom. When I came to another parking lot at the school, I pulled into a stall and broke down. I was sobbing. What the hell was going on? I could feel it, and the girls could feel it. What was so wrong in our lives that my baby girl had pushed an older boy so hard that his head had hit the concrete? Emmett and I had never used physical punishment—I don't think either of the twins had ever even been spanked!

In that parking lot that day, I texted about ten members of my family, begging them to pray for us. Whatever was going wrong, it wouldn't hurt to have a few of the people I loved praying for our family. I don't think anyone knew how to respond…but the vagueness of my text clearly freaked out everyone! They texted me back demanding more details, the very thing I didn't have: details about what was wrong. My brother Josh asked, "What the crap is going on?" I texted him back, "I really don't know. I think Emmett is trying to figure out what he really wants in life…

and I need him to choose us!"

After I sent out those cries for help, we went home and I put all the kids down for naps. I sat staring at the wall all during naptime. What was wrong? Why did my whole body feel as if it were in a constant panic?

Around dinnertime, a fight broke out over a toy, and within minutes, Bailey was nowhere to be found. I looked in every nook and cranny of the house. She wasn't anywhere. I started to freak out. I finally found her outside, around the side of the house hiding behind the garbage cans. "Mom, I have been sitting out here, thinking about running away. What is happening?...What is wrong with us?...Why do I feel so scared?" I wished I had an answer for her. "I'm not sure, Bay," I answered, "but I'm trying to figure all this out too. I am scared too. I feel it just like you do."

I walked into the house, grabbed my car keys, loaded all five kids into the car and drove away. I didn't know where we were going, but we had to get out of that house. I stopped at the home of my brother, Jeff, praying someone would be there so we could go sit in their home and feel the spirit that was always so strong there. I pounded on the front door...but nobody answered. I didn't want to leave. I just stood there with my head against the door, holding onto the handle.

I stood on Jeff's porch probably a good five minutes before I went back to join my crew in the car. I went through every rational idea about what could be wrong...then I tiptoed into the irrational parts of my brain, and began hallucinating about anything and everything that these horrible feelings we were experiencing could mean.

By the time I snapped out of my daze and got back into the car, the baby was screaming. I didn't want to go back home and face the turmoil stirring in the air there. So we drove. Within fifteen minutes, I found my car parked in the parking lot of the LDS temple. The building looked amazing. It was glowing. The kids were patiently watching a movie in the back of the car, so I just soaked up the spirit I felt enveloping me.

I offered a silent prayer, "Heavenly Father, I know you are here. I can feel so much peace just sitting and staring at this beautiful temple. My home is in a state of turmoil. My kids feel it. I feel it. We are scared. I keep having dreams that my baby boy will die. I can't help but wonder if these dreams are preparing me for something. Please help me to find answers about this disturbing power that seems to be settling in on everyone in my family. What is going on?"

A feeling of calmness and quiet reassurance surrounded me and seemed to say, "Be still . . ." I thought that reassuring feeling was an announcement that everything was going to be okay. I didn't realize it at the time, but that encouragement to be calm would be the most important message that would ever come to my mind.

The kids began to get restless. Bostyn had the idea that we should all walk around the temple. We looked like a crew of homeless beggars, but I didn't care. It was nice to be surrounded by the calm feelings that were so strong on the temple grounds.

When we got near the temple, Teage asked if he could walk over and touch the wall. Then the twins began to run towards it. Kaleeya and I soon joined them. With Tytus in my arms and my other four babies by my side...we stood and touched the wall of the temple. In spite of the chilly, wintery air, we quickly felt warm. Nobody said any words, but the stillness that surrounded us spoke to our fears. My children's faith buoyed me up in that moment, one I will never forget. A moment where I stood and felt peace with every fiber of my being. A moment of pure strength and love.

My mind returned to the present as my mother drove with me to take the twins to school. Now, we knew exactly what had been wrong that day just a few weeks ago. But on this day, the girls were excited and nervous to go back to their classroom. They had missed class pictures a few days earlier, but they couldn't wait to have the photo of their classmates—a photograph without them in it. They were not there standing alongside their friends. It was a photo they would later hang up in their room...and every time I passed by, it was a constant reminder that life had stopped for them. They had missed a part of their childhood. They weren't there smiling on that picture day. No, that day, they were home recalling how happy their lives used to be.

We finally pulled up to the school. My heart dropped…I couldn't send them to school. The thought crossed my mind to just turn around and keep driving. Back to our house…the house which no longer had that lingering feeling of some unknown anxiety. The only feeling in our house now, was one of emptiness. But at least in that empty house, I felt that my children were safe from the rest of the world. I could protect them from the hurtful words that would be spoken. I could shelter them from the information about their father's murder, which just a short time later, their classmates would share with them: exactly where the bullets had entered Daddy's body, how many bullets were fired, exactly where the shooting took place in the Walgreens parking lot…that he was on a date with the "bad guy's" wife. These were not the descriptive details I would have shared with my five-year-old girls, but they were details they would come to learn once they were back at school.

We sat in the car for a minute, in silence. How could I let them take this step back into reality? Why did they seem excited and insist that they would be okay? I knew this day would be hard for all of us. What if a bad guy came and took them away? What if people were mean to them? What if they felt alone, and I wasn't there to hold them when they cried?

Finally, the car door opened and I somehow found myself unbuckling my girls, grabbing their hands, and slowly making our way up to the front doors of the school. My eyes burned with tears that threatened to fall down my face. I was shaking and squeezing their hands so hard. We walked into the office and I checked them in. They gave me kisses and headed off to class. Why were they being so brave?

The tears started to fall as I exited the school, and headed to my car. I walked towards it slowly, and then looked up. Parked right in front of my car was a police car! I freaked out. My mind automatically went into a state of shock. Even though I could hardly breathe, I began screaming and I ran as fast as I could back into the office. I was hysterical! "What is... going on? Is there... someone... in the... school? Is there an emergency? Did someone... come... here with a... gun?" Every possible scenario raced through my mind and expressed itself through my frantic screams.

The woman in the front office helped to calm me down. Then a police officer came inside to explain to me why they were there. All of the students at both schools—where our children were enrolled and where Rob and Kandi's children attended—were having a very difficult time. Since the shooting, the police officers had been stopping by the schools daily to check up on everyone, provide reassurance, and hold assemblies to help the children understand and help the kids from both families who would be returning to school. As angry as I was that all of this was actually real, I was also relieved to know that the students were being prepared to help support my grieving daughters.

A few hours later, I got a call from the school. My girls were in the counselor's office and couldn't be consoled by anyone. I raced back to the school to pick them up. They didn't want to talk in the office, so I checked them out and we returned to the car.

The car was silent for the first half of the drive. I kept looking back at them, but they just stared at their feet. Finally, Bostyn decided to speak. "Mom, I'm sorry we didn't stay at school." I tried to be strong. Oh how I wished Emmett were here to protect her, to help me protect her. I thought about the time when Bostyn had been in the hospital because a cut on her eye had become infected. Emmett had stayed with her every minute she lay in that hospital bed. For almost three weeks, he missed school and work and held her while the doctors tried to figure out how to get her better. He had always been there to protect her when she was hurt. Now, it was just me.

"Baby... it's... okay. I am glad you are with me now.... I don't know that I was as ready as you two... for you to go back to school."

"Mom... everything was good. It seemed like a normal day for a while. Then at recess... some boys came over and started telling us how they saw our dad on the news. They were all laughing and saying how cool it was that Daddy got shot in the head.... Did he really get shot in the head and the heart? Those boys are stupid. They don't know anything. They think our life is like a movie. They think that guns are awesome and that we are lucky. We aren't lucky, Mom. The world didn't stop, Mom... but why does it feel like it stopped to me? This isn't something fun! Why are they so stupid? They don't know anything. I never want to go to school again!"

All the horrible things I had wanted to protect them from... over! "Baby... I can't imagine how hard that was for you. I know you probably don't feel like you ever want to go back again... and that is okay for today. People can be mean. *Our* world felt like it was not moving... but everyone else has just been going on with life. Maybe those boys weren't trying to hurt you. I think maybe they probably didn't know what to say to you. They haven't been where we are right now. They don't understand how real this has been for you. To them it *was* like in a movie. They saw it on TV... but they didn't have to feel how it felt for you."

We sat in the driveway for a while and talked about the world. How unfair life seemed. How unreal the past few weeks had felt. That day— the week before their daddy died—that we had spent at the temple. We talked about other people's words and how they can make us feel. We spoke about the words we have said to others... that may have hurt them.

"Can't we just go back and touch the temple? Maybe we can live there?"

And so we went back to our spot on the side of the temple. We held our hands on it again... and felt the power that was inside. We didn't move in, we didn't stay forever... but we did see the hand of the Lord comfort us in that moment, reassuring us that no matter what happened in the world... He still loved us.

We have to be *in* the world...but we don't have to be *of* the world. There are times when darkness surrounds us. Maybe it's in the words others say, maybe it's just a feeling in our hearts that something is wrong. The world tells us we have to be ruthless...that we have to fight to the death. We were suffering the aftershocks of that approach...and it hadn't brought happiness to anyone. The world cries at us to seek revenge, to find others' mistakes and magnify them...and never let them go. The world tells us to hang onto all our pain.

We can't wrap ourselves—or our children—in a plastic bubble of protection. Trust me, I have tried. We are here on earth to go through pain. It sucks. It hurts. It tries to tear us down. We just want to shelter ourselves and our little ones from anything that goes against light, but even when we try with all of our might, darkness will find us. But, we can't just sit silent in the darkness...we have to fight to get back into the light. We can teach our children about faith. We can teach them to be stronger than the hurtful words of others. I wanted to go sit those boys down and scream at them at the top of my lungs. But if it wasn't the ignorance of those boys that day...it would have been something else.

Each day, we have struggles. It wasn't my job to make those boys suffer for the pain they caused my daughters. It was *my* job to comfort my babies and help them see that, although the hardness of the world is all around them, there is also beauty and peace to be found. We need to teach our children to be strong...not to be mean. They will be wronged, and our job is to show them how to forgive. They will be hurt...and we must teach them the ways to find freedom from their pain. Clouds will rage around them...and we must have the strength to show them how to stand strong in the storms. We need to teach them to find goodness in the motives of others...not to seek a bad guy in everyone they meet. "Bad guys" will teach them that the world is ugly. ...We will have to lead them to a world where only God can be their guide. We need to show them to trust...but also to follow the silent whisperings that will speak to their hearts when they are not safe. We have to allow our babies to be in the world…but we want them to rise above the darkness and be pillars of light to the world.

Until we have walked in others' shoes, we cannot truly understand how they feel. We have no way of seeing the pain they carry. Their struggles are unique, and only *they* know what it is that weighs them down. We all have our own challenges to bear. We crave the love and support from those around us to help us make it through the next step on our path.

It is easy to be afraid when we feel we are doing it all alone, and sometimes, we feel like we need to just sit down and stop trying. We cannot make the world support us, even when are seeking the light, but we *can* look for others who also need what we are seeking. And we *can* make a difference. When you encounter others around you who are struggling… find ways to serve them through their grief.

As we try to help lighten the load of their burdens…we might start to feel less alone as we bear our own. If someone is facing the difficult blessing of raising a special needs child day in and day out…find a way to lighten that ongoing burden. Maybe your neighbor is suffering from cancer…lend him your shoulder for strength. Maybe your co-worker just got dumped by her longtime boyfriend…find a way to be there for her. In our words and through our actions, we can always make a difference.

You are not alone in feeling the weight of the world. My little girls felt the unknown darkness of the world when they got into a fight with those older boys who didn't understand the burden they were carrying. They felt it again when their load was too heavy for them to bear alone, and careless children tore them down. Every single person you meet is carrying his or her own cross. Some of those burdens can be seen, and others we will never be known. Isn't the best solution for us to all carry them together?

It is not our job to find answers for other people in their struggles, it is not theirs to find answers in ours…but I can promise you that when we are there for each other…life here on earth can be blessed with light. We can be the Angels that Heaven is pleading for us to be for each other. Then when the storm clouds come, we can stand—hand in hand—reaching together for the peace we seek…like the love and reassurance my family found as we clasped our hands together and leaned against the House of the Lord. As each of us takes each other by the hand and let Him guide us, we will all stand on sacred ground.

CHAPTER SIXTEEN

Bailed Out

IT WAS A TUESDAY, I THINK...LATE MARCH. My mother encouraged me to get out of the house for a change of scenery. For the first time since everything had happened I was alone in public...at a bookstore trying to find a book on grieving children.

It felt weird and awkward walking around inside the up-beat store. Everyone looked so happy and calm. They seemed to be enjoying the quiet and their own thoughts. Not me! I hated being alone with my thoughts, and especially in a public place where any minute I could lose control.

I peeked around the corner of the next aisle...checking my surroundings carefully so that I could venture forward and hope to remain alone. I had no desire to run into anyone I knew...and I especially didn't want my first time in a public place alone to be the time I ran into HER.

I found the section I was looking for and began leafing through the books. They all seemed so long and had way too much information. Couldn't there just be a Do's and Don'ts list to skim through? A checklist of all the things I needed to be doing as a mother of grieving children? Of course not. It couldn't be that easy. I had children who were—on every level of the expression—out of their minds...scared of life. There wasn't going to be an easy fix or a quick pill to dissolve under their tongues. No way to just let us all sleep it off. Every book I looked through made me feel more and more inadequate for this daunting task.

I had just about given up hope of finding a book that felt right for me, when my cellphone began to ring. I dug through my purse hoping to find it before the ringer stopped. Unfortunately, after I pressed the little green button to accept the call and then held the phone to my ear, I wished that my purse had been a little bit bigger, so that I would not have found my phone in time.

"Ashlee...hey." It was a familiar voice from the AG's office, " I don't know if you heard...but our judge was out of town today during the hearing...and um...well the visiting judge allowed Rob's request for bail to be granted... and...um...his parents have put down the bond money... um...so um...as of right now...he is...UM...out of jail." Out of jail! My mind tried to grasp the words that now churned in my stomach.

"What do you mean? How is that possible? What...he...is...how? How can that be an option? ...What if he comes after me? ...What if he breaks into my house and hurts us? All I know about this man is that he shot and killed my husband a few weeks ago and now you're telling me that he could show up at my doorstep or at my kids' school...and you are all okay with this? Nobody is stopping it? I have no choice in the matter?" I felt utter despair. I had absolutely no control.

"Well if anything...he would just come to your house to tell you he was sorry. See, we found some things in his truck. He knew you had no idea about the affair." From this conversation, I learned about a letter he had written me, that was found on the passenger seat of his truck the night he shot Emmett. He had addressed it to me. He knew my name. It had our home address.... He knew where we lived! Tucked inside the envelope, the letter talked about all he had found out about his wife's affair with my husband. How he wanted *me* to help him figure out how to stop it!

Now I was filled with more questions for Rob, the biggest of all being: *then WHY didn't you just send me the letter that night...instead of waiting for my husband with a loaded gun? I was hurting just like he was. Why couldn't we have worked together to find answers for what was going wrong in our marriages? I had been searching alone. Rob, you weren't the only one in pain.... I was sitting at home feeling it all too.*

In some ways, knowing about the letter made me feel better, but in other ways it just left me with more uncertainty. I was out of my mind by this time. I didn't want him at my doorstep...even if he posted the million dollar bond to my own personal account! I didn't want anything to do with him...and now he was not only out of jail...he was headed back to his home, just a few miles away from mine! He just shot my husband in the head and in the heart...and now he could be anywhere? It didn't seem possible that the criminal justice system could allow this to happen.

I don't recall any more of that conversation. My eyes began spinning around, frantically searching for Rob. My heart was racing. Eventually, I hung up the phone. I hunched over in pain. My body felt like it was going to stop. *NOW? Right now... I am sitting in this book store... alone... and he is out of jail? Maybe driving towards me? He could be here any second. What if he is on his way to find me? What if he comes to my house?*

With that thought, all fears about my own well-being faded into the background. *MY KIDS! They're at home.*

What if he's on his way there?

I couldn't stop pacing the floor. I started dialing my phone. The first person I called was my dad. We had just talked an hour before about the hearing that was to take place. I frantically told him what had just happened. He tried to calm me down and assured me that he would be there for me at any hour of the day or night, that everything would be okay, and that he loved me. It reassured me to know that he would be there for me if I needed him.

I didn't know what Rob would do. All I knew was that I was scared....I knew I had to have a way to protect my family. I called one of Emmett's friends, Weston, who worked for a home security company. I hysterically managed to tell him about Rob being out of jail and how scared I was.

He said, "Ashlee...we will be there soon...and if we have to work until midnight...you will have an alarm system in your house before you go to sleep tonight." And he kept his promise. I think it was around 11:45 p.m. when that alarm system was fully installed and activated for the first time. Miracles of man...safety in my heart. I would spend the majority of my time the next few weeks in my house, with the doors locked, the blinds shut, the alarm on...and my cell phone in my hand.

After calling Weston, I found my way back to my car. Somehow, I managed to drive home. I had to tell my kids! The last thing I needed was for a major event in this case to be told to the girls the next day at school. Unfortunately, they didn't handle the news well...and I questioned my decision about telling them.

For every moment of panic and fear we had experienced in the past three weeks, there were a hundred more now! Taps on my shoulder in the middle of the night. Tears of fear at three a.m. Outbursts of anger towards each other...and at me. Nightmares...endless nightmares. Mine usually startled me awake with the sound of a gunshot.

For one week, Rob didn't even have any stipulations put upon him. He just went home and spent an entire week with his family. The judge had opened up the option for bail, unaware of the fact that it would be taken that very day. No ankle monitoring bracelet...no boundaries...no rules.

Thankfully, a week later, Rob was ordered to wear an ankle monitor, and an order was issued for him to have no contact with me, or the only eye witness at the scene of the crime... his wife. Boundaries were set around our house and my kids' school.

At one point, I called the detectives begging for monitoring devices to be put on both me *and* Kandi so that they could call me if I happened to get in the vicinity of either one of them. That way, I could go about my life without the constant fear of running into them wherever I went. They said that wasn't possible. They probably thought I was crazy for asking, but that made the most sense to me. That would have helped me feel safe in my own skin.

Every time I left the house now, I not only imagined that I would see Rob's mug shot in the crowd, but my heart truly believed he was always close behind me. The picture of his face haunted me in the darkness of the night. I left lights on everywhere and kept the blinds closed. I had nightmares. In one, I woke up in the night to feed the baby, and he was sitting outside my window…watching me. I saw his reflection in the glass of all my windows every time I looked out. This man…this person I didn't even know…somehow had complete power over me. I had no control… and I hated it.

I felt helpless. I felt alone. I felt scared that my fate would be the same as Emmett's…that this "bad guy" whom I pictured in my dreams, would find me in the dark of night in some vacant parking lot. I didn't leave my house at night…hardly ever. While everyone else was asleep, I spent many hours shaking and sweating in full-blown panic attacks. The fear of the unknown once again plagued my soul.

Rob would end up being out of jail until September. The end of March until the middle of September! Six months…wondering if I would see him on the streets. Twenty-five weeks…every day leaving the house with a prayer that today wouldn't be the day we would meet. I was always prepared inside for it to happen…but I wasn't prepared for what I might do.

I learned a lot about patience during those weeks. Patience with the law. Patience for what felt unjust. Patience for my own fears. And patience for the new normal that had been created for me. Patience for a life…I still longed to have. Patience for the day I would once again be blessed to have the 'normal' I craved. Patience for my mind to work properly. I waited for my heart to stop pounding out of my chest. Patience for the joy I still hoped to find again. I waited for the trial…I longed for it to come, so it would be over. So we could finally look at each other face to face. Maybe he would say all the words Emmett never could.

I also learned about patience for the Lord's timing. In my life, He always seemed to be telling me to "be still," and now it was not only a gentle whisper...it was a mandatory plea. I had no choice. I had NO control. Patience would have to become one of my strongest virtues...a quality with which I had not had a lot of experience in my twenty-eight years. Through those six long months...I saw and felt the refining fire of the virtue of patience. Patience in my hope, endurance in my faith.

Sometimes, Heavenly Father sends us little reminders of how we can change to become more like Him. Sometimes, He shouts them from the rooftops. He wants us to become like Him in every way. Submissive, patient, full of love. He has asked us to withstand the challenges of this life with all of these virtues, even when every fear we have ever feared comes true in two shots of a gun. It is definitely more easily said than done. He wants us to surround ourselves with opportunities and with experiences that refine us a little more...step-bystep.

I thought the hardest part of my life came the night of Emmett's death... but it didn't. It wasn't just *that* night that I had to stand tall in my closet...I had to continue to stand tall through the years that followed. It wasn't a one-time event that would shape my character and mold me into the woman that He needed me to become. He needed me to not only say that I would stand tall...He needed me to accept it as a part of who I was.

Rob's release from jail was just that for me: a moment when I had to stand in faith. I had to know that Heavenly Father was going to help me be safe, that He knew I could be strong, and that He was begging me to be still, to truly put my life in his hands. And once I let go of all the control I had left...He was always there with me. He continued to give me the words to comfort everyone around me. He reminded me when I got frustrated, to just sit and hold my grieving children. He sent me Angels in the darkest times of my test of patience. And He bailed me out of the pain I thought would destroy me.

Sometimes, no matter how loud He is crying for us to hear His words...we will miss them. We will make mistakes, and we will fall. I know *I* have made mistakes every day, in one way or another. But when we are as low as we can go, *He* will bail us out. He bailed me out on the way home from the burial when he sent my Aunt Diane to volunteer to drive us back. He paid my bond when I walked into church and someone was always there for me, willing to hold a baby or color a picture with my kids. When I was at all of my lowest points... He always sent the payments of love I needed at the very moment I needed them. He knew I had forgotten how to cook and clean... and He sent inspired willing hands to wipe my tears and clean the fear off my countertops.

Just like Rob's parents, our Heavenly Father sees *our* potential. He sees our worth as His sons and daughters. He will beg *our* judges to give us one more chance... He will sacrifice for us if it means that we will come a little closer to Him... if only to let us know that we are loved, He will pay our bond even when we don't deserve it. He knows that we not only need Him, but that we can't make it through this life without Him. He will do whatever it takes to bail us out of our past. When we let Him in, His son Jesus Christ will take upon Himself our sins and our pains... and He will teach us how to survive through our fears. I know that as He has watched me in patience... I have also grown a little of my own.

Some questions we have in life will only be answered after we show we have the faith to endure. Some may never be answered at all before we die... but no matter who we are... He will always bail us out and carry us when we cannot stand alone.

CHAPTER SEVENTEEN

Footprints in the Sand

WHEN EMMETT DIED, HE HAD MANY CLIENTS whose cases he had just begun working on, or whose cases were not yet completed. These clients called requesting refunds, and it was ultimately my responsibility to decide who would get their money back, or how much of their money should be returned. It freaked me out to decide who among his criminal defense clients should have money withheld. I felt overwhelmed and frightened to refuse anyone their requested full-refund. The last thing I wanted was to upset someone battling a criminal case, and have them come looking for me. Every time I had to go talk about the requests at his office, I worked myself up into a frenzy.

I hated the twenty-five minute drive to his office, alone in my car. I hated going inside the office. I hated how it smelled…exactly the same as every other time I had gone there to see Emmett. It was hard that all the same people worked there…especially because most of them had known about the affair before he even died. Sometimes, I felt mad at them.…It's not like any of this was their fault, but somewhere inside of me…I was angry at them for not warning me.

On one occasion, as I drove towards the office, I felt like a stone-cold zombie. I didn't cry during the entire drive, like I usually did.…I was pissed off. I didn't want to spend any more time away from my kids cleaning up his crap. I didn't want to hear Emmett's name. I didn't want to sign my name by his signature. I didn't want to see his and Kandi's handwriting all over the paperwork…together…taunting me. I didn't want to read any of the labels on the files Kandi had prepared for him. I didn't want to stare at the silly 'i's' she wrote with little hearts replacing the dots. I didn't want to see the paint on Emmett's walls. I had picked those colors. We had spent hours going to Home Depot and Lowes trying to pick the perfect shades so the trim and walls would be the same colors as our house.…Ironically, Emmett had wanted that office to remind him of our home. The paint-job looked so great the first time I had seen it all done…the dark brown trim and the tan walls turned out exactly as we had planned. It was just how we wanted it to be. Now, that paint-job was there to mock me…it stared down at me as a nasty, little reminder of all the plans we had made together…and that now, I was living without him.

I walked into the office that day with a chip on my shoulder. I didn't feel like letting anyone in. I didn't want any sympathy hugs. I was going to get down to business…I was not going to feel…I was not going to think. Just write checks, sign papers and get my butt out of there. I sat down with Emmett's employees and began to talk about these piles of criminal cases. I tried so hard to focus on the task at hand. Luckily, despite my stone-cold demeanor…everyone at the office was very willing to help me. I followed their counsel. They gave me all the facts about each case, and we worked together to decide who to pay and how much each of them should receive.

My mind began to wander back to the last time I had sat in this room.… It was a few days after the shooting. I had to meet with the detectives there to sign some release papers and clean out Emmett's office. They had boxed up a lot of it for me already as they had searched for evidence. I glanced through the boxes. I looked through all of his desk drawers.

Inside one of the drawers was a portrait portfolio of my bridal pictures…I remembered the day it was taken like it was yesterday…I had taken off my shoes in the snow to get the perfect look I wanted for the photos. Man, I loved my dress so much. ... I slammed the album shut and put it in the box.

After I had gone through each drawer, I realized that something was missing. ... I started to panic. Where was our family portrait? At one point, Emmett had a family portrait sitting on his desk. Now, it was nowhere to be found. I went through every square inch of that room. Nothing. I got really emotional and frantically begged everyone to help me in my search. I had detectives and everyone at the office searching high and low for it. I think, in my panic, I even grabbed the shirt of one of the detectives and pretty much yelled at him that the portrait was very important to me... and that I had to have it! It *had* to be there and I wasn't leaving without it.

In the back of my mind, that picture was so symbolic. I needed them to find it... because a part of me truly believed if we could find that portrait in this office—this room filled with all of those lost hours when Emmett wasn't at home, and those nights he had spent here with her—that maybe it somehow meant we *were* worth something to him. My panic wasn't about the stupid frame, the glass, or the piece of paper inside... it was about a fear inside of *me* that needed to be calmed. It was easier for me to be furious about not knowing where the missing portrait was, than it was to blame a dead man for not letting me into his life.

Even after we had searched everywhere... we never found it. During the nights following the search, I spent hours trying to figure out where our family photo had ended up... maybe into evidence? Maybe Kandi hid it from him... maybe he threw it into the dumpster. That lost family photo symbolized the family unit we had lost... and it pulled at every one of my aching heartstrings.

So on this day, I wasn't going to get frustrated about lost photographs. I wasn't going to cry over handwriting on a document. I was going to be strong. I was going to accomplish what I came to do, and I was going to leave. Once we had gone through the entire list of everyone who had called, and the checks had all been signed, I said goodbye and got back into my car. Now, all my bottled-up emotions had even more power. They sat in my throat like a red-hot pepper. However, I was determined *not* to let them win. I drove off even angrier than when I had arrived. This place was stupid! It smelled stupid. It looked dumb. I tried hard to pretend I hated it because of everything that it was...and not for all its reminders of memories and heartache.

Robotically, I drove home. A few times, I screamed out in anger against Kandi or Emmett, but for the most part...my car was silent. By the time I walked in the door at my house, I couldn't feel anything. I felt isolated and numb. I sat on my couch like a brick wall. I watched my kids as they threw their arms around me. I heard their tender voices saying they had missed me. I felt their lips as they kissed my cheeks...but I couldn't feel their love.

Soon, I heard Tytus whimpering over the monitor. I was excited to see his little face, and I ran to get him out of his crib. As I walked into the room, I could hear the strains of music from my iPod, which we always turned on for him when he was sleeping. I walked toward his crib and picked him up. He wasn't all the way awake, so I just held him...to see if he was really ready to get up or to go back to sleep. Within seconds, he was fast asleep in my arms, still swaddled like a little burrito.

The song that was playing ended, and for a moment it was silent. Tytus smelled like baby lotion. His skin was so soft on my face. The music began to play again. I recognized the song. As the first word was sung... all the emotions I had bottled-up all day...suddenly found their voice. As the tears fell...I rocked my sleeping baby boy, and I could feel the love surrounding me. I could not only smell his sweet skin, but I could feel his tender spirit snuggle up close to mine.

Footprints in the Sand, I had sung this song to my babies a million times before. It was one of my favorites. But this day, I didn't just sing it to my sleeping baby boy...I sang it to myself. I bore testimony to my *own* soul that I was not alone. I wasn't rocking my baby without my Heavenly Father by my side. I wasn't driving down to the office alone. I wasn't glancing over paperwork covered in Emmett's and Kandi's handwriting...without Him being there with me. I wasn't even searching for a lost family picture alone in the dark.

Heavenly Father kept trying to tell me, in every way He could, that He was there for me...and even when I tried to shut Him out and pretend that everything inside of me was okay...He knew it wasn't. Even on the days when I truly believed I could do it all by myself...He patiently waited for the moment when I would be humbled, and let Him in again.

He must have felt like He was taking crazy pills at times with me... "Ashlee...we have been over this... I am not going to leave you alone....I can see that in this moment you can't feel Me...but I am here waiting for you to let Me in." Every time I pushed Him away...He sent me gentle reminders that He hadn't deserted me. He was still there...and all I had to do was let Him in. When I slowed down and really listened...His love was everywhere. The words to this song spoke that truth to me once again..."You are not alone...I am still right here."

Those times when we feel like we've been given every chance in the world to let Him in—but we haven't taken them—they aren't over. Even if you have denied those impressions every day of your life...your opportunity has not passed you by.

Satan wants you to think that who you are right now, is all that you can become. He wants you to doubt yourself. He wants you to doubt your faith. He wants you to deny those gentle reminders of Christ's love. He encourages you to give up on your dreams. He wants you to stay right where you are... and be content with being "good enough." He wants you to feel satisfaction in being comfortable. He doesn't want you to push on to a better day. He doesn't want you to put others above yourself. He wants you to enjoy whatever compulsion sounds fun at the moment. He wants you to view yourself as the exception. He hopes you look down on others from a pedestal. He wants you to believe you are a little bit better than everyone else. But then...he hopes you see yourself as worthless, as unworthy, and forgotten. He will find your weaknesses and insecurities every day...and make sure they are drilled into your mind...until you just give up the fight. He wants you to hand over all your power to the things that try to bring you down. He is happy to take it into his own hands. He wants you to lose everything you've ever loved. He wants you to fall on your face...and when you do...he walks away. His plan was simple. If we followed him, we would never feel pain...but that same plan would leave us without joy. His plan was foolproof...but joy is what makes our lives now so special. We didn't want simple. We wanted to grow. We wanted to come to earth to progress. We didn't follow Satan because we saw the potential in ourselves then...and Christ still sees it in us now.

He wants to hear your voice. He is patiently sending you sign after sign that He is waiting for your love...and while He waits, He has a love for you beyond any measure you can comprehend. And it's there with no strings attached, and without expectations. It is there regardless of the mistakes you have made, the choices you have messed up...even the shots you have taken. He loves us all.

Even if you've never even spoken His name, He knows YOURS. He hears your heart and sees all of the goodness that you ARE inside. He has seen every footprint you have made in the sands of your life. He has watched through the hard times...and He has seen all the joy. But in those moments when you feel He has abandoned you, when you look back and see only one set of footprints... it isn't because He has left you alone. It is because He is carrying you.

CHAPTER EIGHTEEN

Give Up

ONE NIGHT, I WENT TO TALK TO Teage as he was getting ready to go to sleep. He was sitting on the bed with a photo book in his hands. He had that look on his face, and I knew it was going to one of those conversations again. Teage was staring at a photo of Emmett holding him on the day he was born. He was gazing at it...longingly. I could tell Teage was not going to open up so I said, "Hey Dude...you doing okay?"

"Mom, did he really die...or did he just leave us?" I could feel my knees go weak. "Teage, yeah...he really died. You were there with me buddy...you saw the box we buried him in. Remember? You decided to go into the playroom during the funeral? That was...he...yes son...he really died."

"Mom, that wasn't Dad...that was a box. It could have been anything inside there. Did you just make that up...to make us feel better that our dad didn't want us anymore? It's okay if you tell me. I've thought a lot about this, and I need to know what is real. You wouldn't let us see in the box...and everybody was acting so strange. I don't understand if that was real, or if he just ran off with Kandi and left me here."

My heart wanted to drop into my feet. How on earth could this little boy have so much anger and so much sadness that he would fabricate this scenario in his four-year-old mind?

"Teage, I know Daddy was having a hard time, and I know you went out a few times with him and Kandi. I can't imagine how that made you feel, or what that makes you think about now, but I can tell you one thing, I wasn't going to give up on him. And he still needs you to believe in him now. He loves you. And regardless of the choices he made before he died…we loved him too. I've tried my best to tell you all that you need to know, and I promise I didn't make up his death to try to help you—or even me—feel better about him not being here. It is okay to be mad, or sad. You can talk to me about any of the emotions this stuff stirs up in you. I've been feeling really angry too, and sometimes I don't know what to do with my anger. It's scary when it's inside of me, and I hope you know that we can do whatever it takes to help you get it out too."

He burst into tears. "Mom, it isn't fair! It isn't fair…it isn't fair that he died. I told you…my dreams were real. When he left on his trip…and I kept waking up screaming because he died. You said everything was going to be okay, Mom! You promised he would come back…but He IS NOT coming BACK! I told you my dreams were real. It wasn't a dream, Mom. It was real…but this time he isn't coming back to us. Why didn't you believe me? My dreams were real. It isn't fair. I miss him, Mom. Why does this have to be real? Why did he have to leave me? It hurts so bad in my heart. I can't breathe at night. Why did he have to leave us? He just gave up…he didn't HAVE to die. Why did he let himself die, Mom? He should have protected himself…he should have run away…he shouldn't have given up on living."

I enveloped him in my arms like a newborn baby. I could feel his whole body shaking. His heart was beating faster than I had ever felt. I looked down at the photograph lying on his bed. What a wonderful day that had been…the day Teage had come into the world. Emmett had never looked more proud: he finally had a son. They were best friends from the very first time they looked into each others' eyes. Emmett had big dreams for our little boy. He wanted him to be a jock. He wanted him to be friends with everyone. He wanted him to be a confident little man. He wanted him to have the perfect life…and now here we were…

We cried and rocked for a while. We talked about death. Teage told me some of his thoughts about why we die. We talked about where we go after we die. We cried about everything in the past we didn't understand... and we talked about how to keep on living. We rocked and rocked... and as I watched him... his anger turned into sadness... and then he was finally calm.

"I'm sorry I yelled at you, Mom. I know that none of this is your fault. I love you so much, and I am so happy that you are here with me now."

I had been missing my sweet little boy. "Son, I love you more than words can say. I never meant for you to go through so much pain. It's

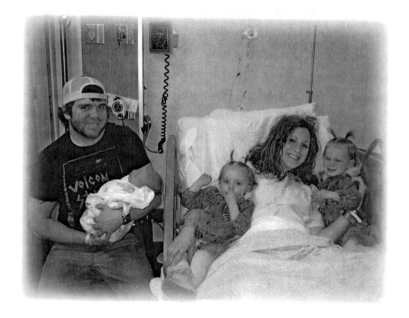

okay to yell at me sometimes if it helps it get out of your head. I have been missing you so much. I've missed your smile, and your laugh... but I will never give up on you because you are mine forever."

It was a difficult ordeal to watch the baby I had rocked just a few years earlier have to think like a man. He had been carrying the weight of a million bricks on his back. I could see it in his face every time he tried to smile. That smile was no longer the "happy boy" grin he used to have. His eyes were always heavy…thoughts always seemed to be churning around inside his mind. And sometimes, he would look at me like he didn't know who to trust. He was just a little kid and yet…he was now the man of the house. He always had such wisdom and knowledge about things I needed to know.

Why did Emmett give up? Why do any of us give up? As far as death goes…we all are going to be there someday, no matter how hard we try to fight it. Emmett didn't have a chance to prevent his death…and now, he no longer had the choice to fight to keep his family…or to give up. We will never know for sure if he would have chosen us…and that hurts.

Emmett didn't know his lie would be discovered. I think he honestly thought he could have it all. He thought he could keep our wonderful life together as a family, while still keeping his secrets. And maybe he could have. I wasn't going to let him go. I had no plans to ever give up on him. Even if he had told me everything, I was prepared to be on his team. All he had to do was tell me. That didn't mean it wasn't going to suck, hurt, and rip out my heart, but I had planned on fighting through it for him.

When we got married, we knew it wouldn't be perfect…no marriage is. But we promised each other we'd hold hands through it all. When we met, I knew instantly that we could make it work. We had each been through the divorces of our own parents, and we had decided to work our butts off to push through our own struggles.

Everyone makes mistakes. Some are life-changing, and others may never make a difference. At some time or another, each of us will be on the side where we are the one in the wrong. If we are willing to love others through their crap…hopefully, they will be there for us when we have a royal screw-up.

The world needs more people who are willing to forgive, repent, and accept their roles. We need to be humble enough to accept forgiveness and move forward in love. Emmett knew I wasn't going to leave. I told him on the day he died I wasn't going to give up on us. But what kept him from telling me the truth? Pride? Fear? Embarrassment? Addiction?

We all have something that holds us back at times, something we constantly put above the relationships in our lives. Adultery. Sex. Food. Cars. Internet. Shopping. Gaming. Work. Friends. Alcohol. Drugs. Pornography. Habits. Exercise. Cell phone. Sleep. ... It can be just about anything. Some of us may have control over these powerful urges... but some of us may have already lost the lives we once lived because of our inability to fight off our impulsive passions. Whatever it is for you... its power is real. It constantly nags at you during every quiet moment... and especially during the loud times in life... begging you to put *it* above all else. Coaxing you to come and join it... and step away from reality.

On occasion, checking-out from life is important: date night with your spouse, girls' night with your roommates, and football games with the guys. But what I am speaking of are those addictions that drive you to abandon your relationships and only focus on THEM. They are powerful tools of deception that keep you from being the person you want to be.

Whatever it is for you, let it go. Find help... beg for it. Let in the people who are all around you. Let them help you find answers for your addictions. Let go of your pride. Let go of your excuses. And plead with God for the courage to fight their drive... before you have no life left.

Find freedom from your addiction to pornography. Let go of the alcohol that puts walls around you and has prevented you from being the type of parent you want to be. Take control of the food that has prevented you from having the healthy body you deserve. Say no to the credit card that calls out to you every second from inside your wallet. Get off your cell phone, and go smooch your husband who just walked in the door from a long day at work. Turn off the football game, and go hold your crying baby so your wife can sit down for a minute of her day. Tell your addiction that you are in charge today, and you be the one to decide if it has a place in your life.

God gives us restrictions because He loves us. He asks us to be responsible for the things we do and say. He wants to empower us by teaching us how to keep all of our strength and not turn it over to the things that attempt to control us. When we follow His counsel, we are free to chose for ourselves and not be enslaved by those addictions that hold us back. Everything suffers when we let our addictions have the power: relationships, work, family, home.

What 'hobbies' are you putting over relationships? What 'passions' are taking over the passion in your marriage? What "need" is driving you away from your children? Something has got to give. Fight for the things worth fighting for and give up those things that add no value to your life. Find balance. Find freedom. Build stable homes. Build them on a foundation that begins with you and God...and you will never be sorry. He wants you to flourish in your relationships. That is the most important work you are here to do, and everything else is just a distraction to try to get you to forget the real reasons you are here.

We only have the power to change ourselves...but when someone around us is struggling...the most powerful tool we have is our love. When Christ sees us struggling, He never stops loving us. Sometimes, He steps back and lets us figure things out...but His love is always there when we are ready for it. To be Christlike, we must learn to have that same type of love. As we see others struggling with addictions...we too can support them with our love. That may not mean that we bail them out, or pay their debts...but that we let them know they have our prayers and that we love them regardless of their current behavior. We can learn that their worth is not connected to their performance...and neither is our love for them. As we pray to find ways to be there for them, we will find answers as to what we can do to support them through their trials.

Each of us has those moments when we stare in the face of someone else's choice that impacts our lives. Those moments may even cause us to give up on ourselves. They may make us want to give up on that person. And in some cases...that will be the answer. No one else will know the answer for what is right for you in your own particular situation... and when those moments come, we must turn to our Heavenly Father. He knows where we have been and He has a destination He wants us to reach. Sometimes, the answer will be to "Be still." Other times, Heavenly Father might inspire us to move on.

At a time in my life when I didn't have any answers...Heavenly Father asked me to "Be still." Then, when all the truths were finally laid out before me...He needed me to move on. I don't know that I will ever understand why it happened this way, but it did. He asked me to have faith. He asked me to believe that He loved me. But most importantly, He asked me to love. He needed me to love Emmett, even when he wasn't worthy of my love. He has asked me to love my kids through some tough days... and oh how I wish I could say I have done it all perfectly. But I haven't... not even a little bit. But I *have* tried my best...and I have asked for His help. And guess what? Even though I have made a million mistakes...He hasn't given up on ME.

No matter where you are...He still loves you. Turn to Him when it's too hard. Beg Him for answers when you feel there are none. Seek His counsel when you are not getting it from anyone else. Strive to be Christlike in all you do and say. Find Christ-like qualities in everyone you meet. When we find a way to cherish each other...to support and love each other and never give up the fight...we will find that Christ will never let us go. He is not going to give up on you...so quit giving up on yourself. You are His forever.

CHAPTER NINETEEN

Choose to be True

EMMETT AND I WERE MARRIED ON MARCH 6, 2004 in the LDS Mount Timpanogos Utah temple. It was a perfect day. Everything was just as we had planned it. The temple ceremony was beautiful. The man who sealed us gave us amazing counsel. The lighting was perfect for pictures. It was a little cold and overcast, but there wasn't a shadow to be seen. I couldn't have been happier. It was surreal standing outside the temple holding hands…as husband and wife.

Afterwards, we had a luncheon at my mother's house for our family and close friends. We had a blast running around the house with all the kids. We were too excited to eat. I remember going into my bedroom one last time and thinking…"This is the beginning of my new life." I stared at all the pictures on the walls. I glanced down at my wedding ring. I thought of all the days I had spent in this room…dreaming about this day. I had planned it all out in my mind…and here I was, living it. I had found the man who loved me enough to want to share his life with me. It was everything I had pictured. Everyone was downstairs.

All of my family. All of his. All of the people who believed in us as a couple and were excited to share this day with us.

Later, we held a reception at the old church featured in the movie *Footloose*. It had been transformed into a reception center, and it was amazing. I loved everything about it. The reception room was exactly as I had always pictured it. We got there early to take photos. Of course...I had mapped out every picture, and had a schedule drawn up for everyone who was to be in each photo. Making my list into a reality was no small task! Emmett was very patient with my craziness. For hours, he smiled through every pose I put him through.

Soon, the guests began to arrive. We had planned on dancing, toasting, and then cutting the cake, but the guests just kept coming. The reception was supposed to be over at around eight o'clock, but the line just kept streaming in. For four hours, a steady stream of people came to show their love and support. We felt like a truly beloved couple. I think between the two of us, each having two sets of parents, and then having moved so many times in our lives, we felt like we and our parents must have known half the world! I loved every minute of it. It was like a little piece of Heaven seeing old faces, meeting new ones...and sharing this special event with the ones who had always been a part of our lives.

It was a perfect night. We finally left the reception center. We hadn't eaten, and we had been on our feet all day. We didn't care. We were like giddy little kids as we laughed in the car all the way to the hotel. After we had checked in, we got into the elevator and were joined by another couple. They told us they had just been married that day, as well. They teased me for still being in my wedding dress...well pretty much every person we passed on the way into the hotel teased me about that. I don't know what I was thinking! I guess I wasn't. All I cared about was the man holding my hand as I got out of the car.

That day, Emmett and I had made many commitments. We had made covenants with each other and with our Heavenly Father to stand true to those commitments. We spent hours that next week on our honeymoon along the Oregon Coast reflecting on the promises we had made. We talked about our fears...and shared our deepest secrets. We cherished every moment we had together. We planned out our future and all that we wanted for our family. We both wanted a lot of kids...we knew that for sure. I came from a huge family and loved everything about it. Emmett was an only child...and he didn't want that same thing for our family. We were on the same wavelength when it came to all of our hopes and dreams. It was easy to love him. I loved being his wife. I couldn't wait to be the mother of his children.

I remember always glancing at his wedding ring and thinking... "Wow...this guy loves me enough...to wear a ring everywhere he goes just to make sure everyone knows he is taken." I loved the feeling that we were only for each other. I loved the safety I saw in that ring on his hand. It was more than just a wedding ring to me, it was a symbol of all the commitments and promises we had made to each other that day...and he wore it proudly.

The night he died...long after the detectives were gone, I remember sitting and staring at that same ring. It sat up on its pedestal on top of our dresser. I couldn't take my eyes off it. It had lost its luster. It didn't shine like it had that day I first put it on his finger. It looked dull. It felt empty...it felt as if I was staring into the face of darkness. I hated that ring for being at my house that night. That ring, which had once symbolized such beauty and love...now just stood there shouting at me..."Guess you weren't enough! Guess all those fears you always had about yourself are all true. Guess you weren't worth it, Ashlee. If you had been, I wouldn't be here right now...I would be on his left ring finger!" But if it had been on his finger, it would have been in a dark body bag.

Emmett taking off his wedding ring was not the first step that got us to where we were. In the beginning, it was just little things. I don't know where it all began for sure, but I really think it started out innocently enough. Then that innocence turned into comfort...and comfort turned into justification. Then there was texting. The texting led to lunch dates...which led to late nights...and eventually, that ring was no longer a reminder of the love he had for me and the promises we had made to each other. For Emmett, it became a reminder of all that he *should* have been cherishing. He didn't take off his ring because he *wanted* to start an affair...he took off that ring because he was too far into the garbage consuming him...that he was ashamed to carry a constant reminder of it on his finger. And for me, I hadn't just wanted him to wear his wedding ring day and night, I had wanted him to come home to me every night...I had wanted him to be there for me every day.

Infidelity starts somewhere...flirty little smiles. Personal text messages. Quick hellos via e-mail. It can happen in a matter of seconds. You let your guard down or show a moment's weakness...and Satan excitedly jumps in to coax you into feeling comfortable with doing just a little bit more. He delights as you walk the line and then stumble and decide it wouldn't hurt to do it just this once. He nudges you a little more...and a little more.

You cannot allow it to begin. Find the strength to say no. Challenge yourself to put on your armor every day as you kiss your loved one good-bye. It is easy to be weak...but it will not bring you joy. Somewhere down the road, the easy road will end, and the joy you once hoped for...will just be a distant memory. Every secret has the power to destroy...even if it is just 'little' secret.

Around every corner lies deception. It is real. It is looking for you. Darkness is just a click away...a send button, an inappropriate conversation. It waits for you to question your commitments...question your decisions.

You *can* be stronger than the world. Satan wants you to believe that everyone is doing it. Just this once won't hurt. Enjoy it. It feels good. Those lies may feel true for that split second...but before that second has the power to destroy you, think about all the moments you will be leaving behind. The moment you knelt at an altar, hand in hand, and made promises to each other. The moment you held your newborn baby in your arms next to the person you loved the most in the entire world. Moments when you look across a messy room full of dirty diapers and an overflowing sink... across the kids' toys and the bills that pile up around you... over to that person you loved enough to commit to... and you realize that you are exactly where you always wanted to be. Those are the moments you risk losing. When you see that person you love, you know without a doubt— even though your spouse drives you insane at times—that he or she is the person for whom you will put on your armor every single day as you leave your home. That is the smile you are going to come home to every night, and you will keep shining that ring... even when the world tells you to just take it off. You are going to put that person first... because you promised God that you would.

You have the power... you have the control. The promises you make to your spouse are not just words. They are covenants with your Heavenly Father. You promise Him that you will cherish and protect His child. There will be temptations everywhere you walk. There will be beautiful things everywhere you look. Find a way to look away... and look to the ones who love you back. True love isn't found in fleeting lustful desires. True love is enduring. It is a dream that each one deserves to come true. When we came to this earth, we knew we would be tested. That moment when you made a commitment to another individual, you never believed your devotion would be tested. But it will. There will always be tests. There will always be trials... in all aspects of our life, and our faithfulness to each other is no exception.

Choose the higher road. Choose the road that leads you back to the promises you have made. In all relationships in our lives, there will be times when we question why we are there. There will be days when we just want to run away... and maybe even take off the symbols that bind us together. Don't take the easy way out! Remember the times when all you could think about was being together. Remember the little things that caused you to fall in love, and fall in love with those things again…and stop focusing on the things that drive you away. Challenge yourself a little more. Be a little more loyal in all you do and say. If something is important to your spouse…do it. If something you do is hurting him or her… stop it. Put your spouse first. Think a little less about yourself. Hold true to the armor that protects you from everything the world will throw at you. Put your family first. If the luster on that ring has become dull…ask Heaven's Angels to bring the polish you need to make it shine again. You have the power to choose…choose to be true.

CHAPTER TWENTY

Capture the Moments

MY FRIEND CHERYL OFFERED TO TAKE PICTURES of the kids for me for Easter. I hadn't taken any photos since Emmett died, so I thought it would be a great idea. I told the kids they would get to hold bunnies on their laps...and they couldn't have been more excited.

As the day of our appointment came, I started to doubt if it was such a good idea. I was still really angry at myself for never having gotten a family portrait taken of us all together after Tytus was born. The only picture of all of us with Tytus was in the hospital. The twins were upset because they wanted to be holding Ty, and it was literally the worst family picture we had ever had taken. I talked about going out and doing some family pictures in the weeks that followed, but we never got around to it before Emmett died. I was so mad at myself. One of my biggest passions in life was capturing moments for other families with my camera...but I had failed to capture my *own* family's moment.

I was nervous all day as I prepared in every way for the kids to be ready and happy for their pictures. Once every one had taken naps, I got them all up and started doing their hair and getting them dressed. My heart hurt. I wasn't sure I wanted to celebrate any holidays this year...and taking Easter pictures of my children without me and Emmett in them seemed so depressing. I didn't really have a "family" to do a family portrait... so it just seemed easier not to take any pictures at all.

I got everyone buckled up in the car. As soon as I turned the key...

panic came over me. How was this happening? I was going to ask my kids to sit in front of a camera and smile...when they had nothing to smile about. How could I ask them to smile at me...when I didn't even know if I was physically able to smile back at them? I pressed down on the pedal...barely. The drive to Cheryl's house should have taken about five minutes...but that day, it took us nearly twenty.

I was overcome by a wave of emotion. I was angry to be a widow. I felt abandoned. I felt alone. I was mad that we didn't have a complete family portrait to hang on our wall. I was overwhelmed by the fact that holidays weren't going to take a year off...life was going to continue, no matter how much my little mind tried to pretend that it wouldn't. I couldn't stop my tears long enough to park and go inside. We passed Cheryl's house a few times as I tried to talk myself into stopping. Each time we came close to it, I would slow down to pull over...but then the tears would start to fall, and I would keep my foot on the accelerator.

Finally, I got my tears to stop. I parked the car and unloaded each one of my babies. They looked amazing. I decided to dress the girls in the white dresses they wore for Emmett's funeral. At the time, I know everyone thought it strange that I put the kids in white instead of black, but I couldn't picture my children dressed in black. I needed each of them to be a light for me...and everyone else who saw them that day.

They walked hand in hand to the door. My tears wanted so badly to keep coming, but I gulped them down. The front door opened. We walked in, and the kids sat down to take off their shoes. They were a bit nervous...like me, they probably also wondered if they had it in them to smile.

We got them all situated in front of the backdrop and began placing bunnies on their laps. For the first time since their dad had died, I saw light in their eyes. They were so excited to see these new little bunnies... animals so full of youth and life. It was as if the bunnies were bringing a little sparkle into my children's empty souls.

I felt tears began to fall as I watched my kids re-discover their smiles. They looked out, each set of blue eyes staring straight at me. *I* was the only one watching. *I* was the only one they had to look to. I saw hope in their eyes...and it was all directed at ME. I had to figure out how to be the best me I could be...because now, I was the only one they had to smile for.

I thought about Easter. What did it mean to me now? I knew it applied to Emmett...he needed Christ to save his soul. I saw how it could help Kandi...she had so many things for which she needed to repent, that it made me want to scream. I knew that Rob would need the Atonement to find forgiveness for pulling that trigger and killing my husband. But I was the victim...why did I need the Atonement? What was Easter going to do for me? From every Easter lesson I had ever heard, the main thing I remembered was that it was for the sinners of the world. Christ had suffered to take away THEIR sins. I wasn't a widow because of *my* sins. I knew exactly why I was here...and it was because of the sins committed by others. Christ's sacrifice on the cross wasn't for me, right? Or was it?

As I watched my babies play with bunnies and giggle as they squirmed... I thought about Christ's promise. He died so that we could all live again. Live with Him. Live with eternal happiness. Live eternally. These smiles for which my children had been searching...could last forever? Yes! They could have eternal happiness...because the Savior died—even for them! He knew they would go through pain. He knew that at some point in their lives, they would lose the glimmer of hope in their eyes, and they would forget how to smile. So He suffered in Gethsemane and hung on the cross for THEM, so that the wounds that had stolen their childhood could be healed. He died so they could smile...eternally.

They were the victims. They were the ones who suffered. Rob didn't suffer to help them heal. Kandi and Emmett didn't go through pain so my children could one day feel whole again...but Christ did. And He did it willingly because He loves us. He agreed to take upon Himself, not only the sinner's pain of regret and remorse, but also the pain suffered by the victims, who were yearning for peace.

All of the sudden, my tears were no longer about the moments I had lost. They were not about the family I no longer had. The tears that filled my eyes as I watched my little ones smile...were tears of joy for all that I *did* have. I had a Savior who not only righted my wrongs when I needed Him to, but who died for me so that I could one day live with Him again. I had a family. I was staring right at them. There were ten tiny hands that needed me to hold them. There were ten big, blue eyes watching me to learn how to keep on living. There were five little hearts beating to inspire my own failing heart. Yes, I had been wronged. Many things were taken from me on the day those bullets were fired...but my family wasn't destroyed. My children still needed me...and even more than that...I needed them. I had a family! And they were perfect.

When the little babies started getting restless, Cheryl asked me to jump in for a shot. I hesitated for a moment. My pride told me that a photo of me in tears next to my beautiful children wouldn't look good. Then I thought of the picture we had never taken with Emmett, and I grabbed my babies in my arms, and red eyes and all, I smiled for all the blessings that surrounded me at that moment. I smiled for my Savior who died for me on the cross so that I could smile forever. I beamed because I was blessed to be the mother of these perfect little spirits who shared my difficult challenge. Yes, we were the victims...but we were smiling.

Easter is a holiday of hope. It is about the love we have for our Savior, who in turn shows us that His love is eternal...and His sacrifice is for us. I *did* believe in Easter. I *knew* the Atonement was real and that I needed its power. For the first time, I saw my children for what they were...my family. They were all I had...and I needed to accept this fact and show them that I could do this with them by my side. I was all they were smiling for now...so I needed to figure out how to be the best, healthiest me I could be.

As we snuggled the bunnies and thought about the true meaning of Easter, I couldn't help but wonder how the Atonement works after we die. What did it still mean for Emmett? I wanted to know that even he could find a way to use the power of the Atonement to heal his soul, because I knew that as he healed…these children would find peace too. We all needed the sacrifice that Christ had made for us. We needed to find peace. We yearned to become whole again. Jesus didn't just suffer and die for Emmett, Kandi and Rob…He died for me as well. He died to help heal my soul. He died so that when I make mistakes, I can be forgiven. The Atonement is real and it is not just for when we sin, but also for when we need to forgive. His power to heal is for all of us. Regardless of what Rob did, regardless of the choices Emmett made before his death, I had a job to do…right now, for ME.

'Capturing the moment' is not always done with a camera…it's also living and breathing in the moments we stand…the moments we've been given here on earth. It's finding joy right where we are in life, and not waiting for tomorrow to bring us the happiness we seek. We must capture the moments when we stand! We can't let them pass us by. We must capture them in our minds…capture them in ours hearts and capture them with the ones we love. We must feel with every fiber…the moments we are living right now. We must believe in our hearts that Christ not only died for us in our sins…but that He also died to heal us in the moments when others' sins have shattered us.

I didn't get the family picture I always wanted, but I *was* blessed with the ability to picture the life I had right now and cherish the blessings all around me. Christ had not forgotten about me. He had not given up on my family. He was proud of us and wanted me to be proud of the family I was raising. We weren't broken…because He would heal us. We were a family…just the way we were.

The Atonement is not just for someone who has sinned…it is for all the victims—young or old—who are smiling through their pain, all the souls who feel abandoned and unlovable. It is for every single one of us to capture in our hearts and hold onto forever. Even in moments when we have turned away from Him, or we cannot see how His sacrifice applies to us, He is still there to take upon Himself our pain. That day, I smiled for every hope I had in the Atonement, which I needed now more than ever before. The Atonement was for ME. Easter had meaning…and it meant that one-day, I *would* feel whole again. And in that moment, I knew that Christ sees us as being everything He ever wanted us to be. He had taken our pain upon Himself, and only He can provide the light to make us whole again.

CHAPTER TWENTY-ONE

Say Something

MY FRIEND JEN INVITED TEAGE TO GO to her preschool three days a week. She knew it was a way she could help him...and it did. It got him out and involved in something. He enjoyed it, and more and more often, he came home talking about what they were doing and about his new friends. Teage had never gone to preschool away from home before, so it was all so new and exciting for him. At the end of the session, Jen invited him to participate in the end-of-the-year performance for all the families to come and see what the children had learned throughout the year.

Teage talked about it for days—how awesome it would be to get up with his class and sing all the songs they had shared with him. He anticipated the day of the program and couldn't wait to go up and show me all that he had learned in his few short months of preschool.

The day of the performance came. As he walked toward the door he was so excited, he was skipping. He couldn't wait to stand up in front with all of his friends and sing his heart out to me. We went inside, and began talking with some of the other parents and kids. After a few minutes, I could see that 'look' coming into his eyes. He started glancing around the room like he didn't know where he was, his eyes shifting quickly back and forth. He was no longer skipping and jumping around with all of the other kids. He didn't move anything but his eyes...and they circled the room...while his body remained still.

I sat there wondering what he was thinking about and what had taken away the enthusiastic smile he had worn the whole way there. Finally, he came and stood by me and grabbed my hand. I looked down to see if he was okay. He had tears in his eyes. I knelt down beside him and said, "Hey dude…I can't wait to see you sing your songs. Is everything okay?" Alligator tears came streaming down his cheeks. "So Mom…why am I the only kid in this room who doesn't have a dad?" He let go of my hand and ran into the bathroom and slammed the door.

I followed. I knocked on the door. He didn't answer. I knocked a few more times…but no reply. So, I slowly turned the handle. As I peeked inside, I could see him lying on the floor sobbing. I shut the door behind me. "Hey bud…I am so sorry," I said. "I can't do it, Mom!" he replied. "Why isn't he here for this? Why can't he just come and watch? He can go back in the box after it's over…but I am *not* going up there unless he is here to tell me how proud he is of me."

I lay down on the floor next to him and stared up at the ceiling. I could see all the texture in the paint. I could hear all the dads laughing out in the hallway. I so wanted to just pick Teage up and make him go up and sing for ME…but instead, we just lay there together. "It's okay, buddy. I would much rather lie right here with you tonight." He grabbed my hand and we lay there quiet and still. We listened to all the songs the kids sang. We could hear the dads clap and cheer as each song ended. We could hear them saying how proud they were of their children. I could feel Teage's hand squeeze mine tighter every time a song ended…and his eyes continued to leak like a faucet. Every once in a while, I would take my hand and wipe away his tears. We didn't say any words to each other…

With Teage's hand in mine, I longed to tell him that everything was going to be okay…even that I could understand what he was going through…but I couldn't…so I didn't say a word. Emmett wasn't there. I couldn't hear *him* outside the door cheering. I couldn't see *his* hands clapping for Teage…but I *could* feel that he was looking down on us, watching as our tears fell onto the tile and knowing that our hearts longed to hear his voice. It was as if Teage were waiting for his father to come and pick him up and say all the words he longed to hear.

There is a song I have recently come to love. It has many meanings to me... *Say Something.*

I can almost picture Teage's little heart singing that song as he lay frozen on the cold bathroom floor that day. He was waiting for Emmett to say something...to remind him that he was there watching him. He was waiting for his father to show up and clap for him. He longed to hear Emmett shout out—when a song ended—that he was proud of him. But instead of waiting out in front of the audience where Teage could watch for him...we waited on the floor with the door shut. He knew his dad wouldn't be there that day...but he waited anyway. As loud as Teage's voice could sing—even if Emmett could have heard the words where he was—he would never be coming that night. We both knew it...but hand in hand, we waited to hear him say something.

There will be days when we feel like we might as well just give up... when we know darn well that the voices we long to hear or the words we seek will never come. We give up on our dreams...and give up on ourselves. We give up on others we hope will change. There will be moments when we are lying on the bathroom floor waiting for someone to hear our cries...or waiting for someone to speak to us. Maybe we're hoping our Heavenly Father will be listening. Our souls are crying up to Him..."Hey...please say something! I am starting to give up on you. Please come and give me answers to all that I've been begging for. Please let me know you are here...'cause I feel so alone. Please say something... because I'm beginning to wonder if you care."

Maybe we are just waiting for a sliver of relief from a physical pain that overwhelms us every minute of every day. For some, we wait for the life we feel we deserve. Some of us have goals we are waiting to attain. Others wait for exam results to determine what their future plans will be.

Sometimes we wait for someone to encourage us...when we feel we have no more fight in us to keep going. We will all have to wait...sometimes for ourselves, sometimes for the people we love, and sometimes, we will be waiting for God.

In those moments, we plead to hear what we've been longing for. I think there are days when Heavenly Father looks at us in the same way. "Hey...you. I'm starting to lose hope that you'll ever say anything to me. I've followed you everywhere. I am not giving up on you...but please say something! Ask me for what it is you need. Let me know what you are thankful for. I don't care what you say...but I am here...just say something to let me know that you know that...I am here."

We are *all* going to feel alone. We are not going to reach all of our goals. We are going to stumble and fall. Sometimes we are going to feel alone lying on a bathroom floor while everything around us moves along perfectly.

Teage was probably waiting for me, in a lot of ways that night, to tell him all the words he needed to hear...but those words never came. We sat in silence...

Sometimes we will be blessed with the words to say, and other times...we will be blessed with the peace to just lie down and be there for someone.

There were a few people who showed up at my house the day after Emmett died who did just that for me. They didn't come with grand words or marvelous insights to try to help me find my way. They just held me and cried with me. But their silence spoke volumes to my soul. Their arms around me gave me strength to reach out to the next soul who came to find some light from me. Their silence whispered love to my heart, and brought peace to my mind.

Silence can feel scary. But sometimes, as we shut out the sounds around us...those are the moments when we feel true beauty. We feel real peace. When darkness tries to settle in your heart...shut off the noises all around you...and listen to the silence. Let your heart feel the calm, and without words, you will feel God's love. He will grab you by the hand and lie down on the cold hard floor with you. He will wipe your tears. He might not come with mighty words...or the answers you seek...but He will send his love, and in that moment, you will know, without a doubt, that He is real.

Sometimes the moment when you are waiting for Him to say something...is actually the time when silence brings true peace to your soul.

CHAPTER TWENTY-TWO

Death and Taxes

I REMEMBER EXACTLY WHERE I WAS IN Sixth Grade when, for the first time, I heard the saying, "Death and taxes." I was sitting in my mom's bedroom trying to explain to her why I wanted 'out' of something I was supposed to do. She was reminding me that although she was very aware of the fact that I didn't *have* to do anything…some things are inevitable. She taught me the concept that—in spite of our desires to the contrary—every citizen of the United States will have to pay taxes…and each of us will one day die. Paying taxes was a concept that was very far away for me, and at that time in my life…death was just a word.

Neither of those things seemed like something I would ever have to worry about. I didn't realize the truthfulness of her lesson, but I loved the power that came from her words. There weren't many things in life I *had* to do. It was kind of exciting thinking of life that way… feeling the power of my own strength.

Before Emmett's death, our family had already come to feel the pain of death…but taxes had not been something I had put much energy into. They were always taken care of for me. Emmett handled most of the business side of our family obligations. I really had no idea of what I had to do in that area.

After Emmett died and springtime came…I found myself facing tax season on my own. At first, I was overwhelmed, but luckily Emmett had been very organized and our accountant already had everything he needed to file my taxes for me. We had been in contact many times, and I hadn't had to think a lot about it. It was a miracle. I was relieved that this part of my journey alone seemed to be fairly simple.

One day my phone rang. It was our accountant. "Hey Ashlee," he said, "this is Rick Sager. I...um...so since Kandi was an employee of Emmett's, technically, now that Emmett is gone...she is in there...as one of your employees. In 2010, she worked for you guys. So, I have tried with all my might to contact someone who can change this...but...but...uh, I can't get you out of it...and I know you already have so much on your plate... but legally...man, I feel like I'm pouring salt into your wounds...but I'm going to need you to write a big check for her employee taxes for 2010. That's the only thing left for us to do. Emmett had given me everything else that an employer does for an employee, but he hadn't yet written that check. I am so sorry. I have tried everything to avoid this call...but I don't think there is any way around it. Legally as her employer...her employee taxes have to be paid by you. I will need a check within the week to pay Kandi's employee taxes. And unfortunately, you will have to do it again next year for this year's taxes as well."

I felt like a trapped baby deer surrounded by hunters. I didn't even know what to begin to say. I tried to wrap my mind around the fact that I had all this anger towards this woman...and now I had to pay her taxes as well! I felt sick to my stomach. Hadn't I already given up enough for her? Weren't the sacrifices I had already made for her sufficient for all eternity? Couldn't she just pay her own taxes? There had to be an easier way out of this one. Someone *had* to listen to my story and feel my pain...and find a solution for me. There was no way I could do this...and I shouldn't *have* to.

I stewed about it for days. I was pissed off! I didn't deserve this. I had already given up enough for Kandi. I made up my mind that I would not be paying those taxes...even if the IRS themselves came to my door. It was not going to happen! I did some online research. I called some of Emmett's attorney friends. I even contacted the IRS myself, but the more

I sought for a way out…the more I tried to find a loophole…the more I realized there was no way around it. I would have to pay those taxes. I would have to write that check.

Heavenly Father couldn't bail me out of this one. There are only two things in this world we cannot get out of…death…and taxes. I had known that for years. However, I never realized how true it was until I was forced to pay the taxes for a woman…a woman who was sleeping with my husband! A woman whose husband had shot and killed mine. In *my* mind, *she* was the reason I was a widow. *She* was the one who had put herself between two men…forcing their confrontation. *She* was the reason I was in this situation, and now…they were asking me to take money… money I needed to support my children…to sacrifice for *HER*? I was angry. I felt sorry for myself. I felt like everything that had already been unjust and unfair…had reached the very pinnacle of total absurdity. It was inhumane! It wasn't about the amount of money, but it *was* about the principle. I shouldn't have to suffer or sacrifice anything more for *HER*!

I didn't sleep well for a few nights. I huffed and puffed and tried with all of my heart to figure my way out the mess. One night, after I had tucked my kids into bed, I went to the computer to do more research to find my "easy out clause." As I sat in my chair, a paper fell out of the basket right above my head. I picked it up. It was a sheet of quotes my sister had given me. She had received it from an Institute class on a night when I was struggling because Emmett had left on a trip before his death. The quotes were all about forgiveness…a long list of quotes.

"And blessed are the peacemakers; for they shall be called the children of God." (*King James Bible: Matthew 5:9*).

"Ye have heard that it hath been said, An eye for an eye, and a tooth for a tooth: But I say unto you, That ye resist not evil: but whosoever shall smite thee on thy right cheek, turn to him the other also. And if any man will sue thee at the law, and take away thy coat, let him have *thy* cloak also. And whosoever shall compel thee to go a mile, go with him twain. Give to him that asketh thee, and from him that would borrow of thee turn not thou away." (*King James Bible: Matthew 5:38-42*).

"Cry. Forgive. Learn. Move on. Let your tears water the seeds of your future happiness."

"Forbearing one another, and forgiving one another, if any man have a quarrel against any: even as Christ forgave you, so also do ye." (*King James Bible: Colossians 3:13*).

"But if ye forgive not men their trespasses, neither will your Father forgive your trespasses." (*King James Bible: Matthew 6:15*).

"But I say unto you, Love your enemies, bless them that curse you, do good to them that hate you, and pray for them which despitefully use you, and persecute you;" (*King James Bible: Matthew 5:44*).

"But I say unto you, that ye shall not resist evil, but whosoever shall smite thee on thy right cheek, turn to him the other also;" (*Book of Mormon: 3 Nephi 12:39*).

It felt so simple... so certain. It was as if God had come and grabbed my bullheaded little face and said, "Ash... AGAIN... this is not about... YOU. I have asked you to walk in faith. I have seen that you have been wronged. I can see that you are hurting. I am so sorry... but I need you to not only have faith in me, I need you to turn the other cheek." I knew what I had to do.

I opened up the cupboard and grabbed my checkbook. I got a pen from the drawer. I opened up to a clean, blank check, and I began to write. Writing that check... in that moment... felt like I was being asked to give up my firstborn child. My heart pounded with every movement of my pen. I was angry at her for all she had done to my family. I was angry that she was the one he had chosen that horrible night. I hated that I *HAD* to write that check... but I knew I could do it. Something stronger than me had given me the ability to do it. I signed that check, with regret, but I also signed it with faith.

He wasn't asking me to pay those taxes for anyone but Him. I wrote that check, not for Rick ... not for Kandi ... not for the IRS ... and not even for myself. I wrote that check for God. I wrote each number one by one ... because HE asked me to. Heavenly Father knew how hard it was going to be for me to write it. He watched me. He felt my pain that day. He saw the money leave my hand ... to go to pay for HER. He knew it wouldn't be easy. He never promised that it would be, but it was a sacrifice I could make ... because I loved HIM.

I didn't deserve to have to sacrifice for her, but I did it anyway. I did it for Christ. Our Savior didn't deserve to sacrifice for me, but He did it because our Father had asked him to ... and He loved His Son ... and He loves me. None of us are exempt from the pain of this world. There will not always be an easy way out. But through Christ, the pain can feel less excruciating. His love can show us the path that will lead us back to Him. He knew I needed Him to help me find the faith I needed, before that sacrifice could truly be for Him.

We will all make sacrifices. We will all be asked to give something up in a moment when we feel abused and used. We won't know until we are there—in that moment—what those hard things will be. It might come when we feel prepared ... but, it will probably come when we least expect it. We don't have to do it alone. We might as well do it for Him, because if we don't, it will all be in vain. It will all be for nothing if we are not doing it with *Him* on our team. I could have written that check the first time I was asked. I could have done it because of my faith in the law ... but that faith didn't give me the strength to do it. I needed more than just the will to do what was legally right. I needed the comfort to know that my sacrifice was more than just for her.

We will have responsibilities that are so hard . . but we can do them. And when we do them for Christ, they will be sacrifices He will never forget. No sacrifice, big or small will go unnoticed. Christ is the author and finisher of our faith. In all that we do, we must do it for Him. And when we do, He will give us the strength to keep going during the difficult moments of our lives. We will find that our faith is stronger because it has been refined.

Even in our daily challenges—changing a diaper, making a bed, cleaning hair left in the drain by our roommates, driving to a job we don't like, making our meals, waving at the neighbor who never waves back— we must devote ourselves to doing all things for Him. Pray that even when it feels too hard to get out of bed…you will have the strength and courage to get up for Him, because on some days…He will be the only one who cares if you do.

I wanted so badly to be the exception that day. I searched for someone to get me out of it. It WASN'T fair. I had suffered enough. I wanted to run away from all the pain I had suffered, but instead…I was asked to turn the other cheek.

"I, the Lord, will forgive whom I will forgive, but of you it is required to forgive all men." (*Doctrine and Covenants 64:10*).

All men! In that bold declaration made by our Father to us all…there was no "with the exception of" or an "unless of course!" His plea for us to forgive wasn't written with an: "except for you Ashlee. You are the exception." He asked us to forgive ALL men…every time, even the ones who might have wronged us and have never asked for our forgiveness. Even when it feels like they don't care or see our pain. Even the ones who have left a hole in our lives with a single blow.….*All* men.

Writing that check that day was another big stepping stone for me. It was a moment when I felt like I should have been bailed out…but instead of giving me a "get out of jail free" card that day, God sent His words to remind me of why I was being asked to sacrifice for Him. He reminded me that I was not forgotten…that He knew I would have to do hard things… but that I could be strong enough to let it go, and blindly obey in faith. I don't know if I will ever SEE any good from writing that check, but I have felt the power that came from obeying my Father in Heaven.

There are some things in life we cannot control…death and taxes…

but we still hold power over the rest. We have the power to choose who we want to be. Don't let your fears keep you from living the life you have always dreamed you would have. Don't let your fear of being taxed hold you back from all the moments where signing the check helps you realize that you have faith in more than yourself. Don't let your fear of dying... keep you from living. If we fear the things we cannot control, they will control us. Let them go.

In those moments when the universe seems to be giving you the last drop you can hold in your vessel...turn to Him. The sacrifices you make are hard, they are overwhelming, they are annoying...and sometimes, they cause unbearable pain. You don't have to make them alone. Turn to Him. Lean on Him when you feel you can't take one more thing...on your own. He will not leave you. I promise you He is there. Let the light of Christ cross your 't's' and dot your 'i's' when the taxes of life are thrown in your face...and when you sign your signature on the bottom of all the big checks, His name will be right there too. It will still be hard...but YOU will never be alone as you make those sacrifices.

CHAPTER TWENTY-THREE

The Gift

I REMEMBER WANTING TO GO TO THE temple. I knew the peace I would feel inside would be like no other I could feel on earth. The darkness that always seemed to be weighing heavily on me would not be allowed to come inside the Lord's House. I finally scheduled a day to go with my sister, Abbey, and my mother.

That morning, Teage was having an extra-hard time. He was clinging to my arm, and I could hardly get ready. I felt that I needed to be home with him, but I also knew that the blessing of serving in the temple would help me be a better parent for him.

I explained to him that it would be okay, that I wanted to go to the temple to learn how to be a better mom for him. He seemed to calm down for a moment, but then as I walked to the door to leave, Teage became hysterical. "Please," he screamed, "you can't leave me! I need you to stay here with me, MOM. Please don't go...I need you here...what if someone shoots you! Please don't leave me here, Mom....Please stay!" He grabbed onto my leg, making it impossible for me to take another step. I didn't know what to do. I was torn between my opportunity to go to the temple...and my screaming boy who wouldn't let me go. Both were important.

I sat there trying to figure out what I should do...an internal battle for which choice was the best. All of the sudden, my Mom grabbed his hand and said, "Teage...I have been thinking about you all day...and I really want to have some time with you. Your mom needs to be in the temple today...but I feel like being here with you is just where I need to be." He jumped into her arms and snuggled into her shoulder. She was inspired. I knew I needed to be in the temple that day… and she knew that *he* needed her there.

Abbey and I kissed him and the other children, and then hopped into the car. She drove. My heart still hurt leaving Teage behind, knowing he was having such a hard time… but I knew where I needed to be that morning. The last time I had been in the temple, I had been all alone… praying for answers to help my family. Emmett was on his trip. And now, even though I wasn't driving there by myself… I felt more alone than words can even describe.

I knew that today was going to be emotional for me, but I thought I would be able to be strong… at least until we got into the celestial room. I knew the tears would hit in there. We pulled away from the house. Abbey had a CD playing in her car. I had never heard the song before, so I just listened to the words while she sang quietly along with them. He voice was soft, but she still sang with all her heart. Just as it had been many times before for me, Abbey's voice was like a peaceful breeze calming my mind. Every word that played… and she sang… spoke to my heart. I am not sure if it was the words of the song… or my sister's love, but I burst into tears.

Live like you Believe

(used with permission from Jenny Philips and Tyler Castleton)

You have felt the warmth of the fire

You have seen a glimmer of light

It's something that you have been missing inside

Something that you have been longing to find

Hold on to the yearning

And wherever you are on your journey

Live like you believe

Live like you know

It's one sure way

Your faith will grow

Listen to your heart

Search in your soul

And you'll find

The strength that you need

His light, the gift of His peace

When you live like you believe

There are things you'll have to let go

And you might feel, you're just hanging on

When you find yourself alone and afraid

Questioning all the choices you've made

Hold on to the burning

He's leading you on through the journey

Live like you believe

Live like you know

It's one sure way

Your faith will grow

Listen to your heart

Search in your soul

And you'll find

The strength that you need

His light, the gift of His peace

When you live like you believe

Hold on to the yearning

And wherever you are on the journey . . .

A message that seemed to be written just for me was playing over and over. She set the song to play on repeat. We drove... while tears streamed down my face. I thought of all the times I had gone to the temple in the past. Our wedding day. The many moments we had walked—hand in hand—into the front doors... excited to be together... excited to feel the love we felt so strongly in one of those holy buildings. Every time we had ever even set foot onto the grounds of a temple, it helped me feel stronger in my relationships... with Emmett... with our children... and as a family.

Our very first outing with the twins was to the grounds of the Logan Temple. They were exactly one week old. I loved walking around in the spring sunshine, and Emmett's mother snapped photos to capture our moment. There were flowers everywhere. Everything was so full of life. It was a perfect day for me, my babies, and my husband... standing in one of the Holy Places that made us an eternal family.

Everyone on the temple grounds that day seemed to be watching us with our precious, little gifts who were exploring the beauty of the world for the very first time. That day was a gift to me... a memory I will never forget. The first time I was out in public as a mother was everything I had dreamed of, everything I had hoped for. My little daughters were amazing. Our family had grown... and I was enjoying every second of it.

We were like the *Four Amigos.* Emmett and I each had a baby in our arms. We took them everywhere with us. We were born to be parents... and these beautiful, little twin girls made it fun. They laughed at everything we did. All Emmett had to do was make a funny noise... and they were in hysterics. They thought he was the funniest person ever. I loved the way they looked into his eyes. I loved seeing the love my daughters had for their father.

When the twins were about nine months old, I got called to be the chorister at church. Either I would take one of the girls up in front of the congregation and balance her on my hip while I led the music...or Emmett would have them both sitting with him. It was so fun to look down and watch him trying to juggle our wiggly babies— who could see me, but couldn't have me—as he tried so hard to keep them happy. He did everything he could to get them to stay put. He gave them anything they wanted. The girls had him wrapped around their little fingers. He never wanted to disappoint them. He had a gift to make them laugh...and in those early years, he seemed to live to make them smile.

I remember in the weeks before Emmett died...wondering where that gift had gone. He had lost the sparkle in his eyes and the desire to make us smile and laugh. At the time, I truly believed it was my fault, and I constantly wondered what *I* needed to change about *me* for him to get that gift back into his eyes. I like to think he would have found it again... because it was truly one of his spiritual gifts in life...the ability to make his children smile. They watched him...and they never took their eyes off of him.

Being in the temple that day was no different than the ride there in the car had been. I sobbed. I spent the day...shaking...and sobbing... the whole time. I don't think anyone around me heard a single word said. I have never felt so overcome with peace...and yet so filled with questions and despair. In my mind, I begged for answers as to why everything had ended the way it had. I questioned my future. I tried to sort out... what parts of my past had been real and genuine, and what had been lies. I cried for the memories I had of my little girls on the temple grounds... knowing that one day, when they married, they would have to come to the temple without their father. He wouldn't be there for them when they brought their newborn babes for photos among the flowers on the temple grounds. I sobbed for all the little memories I felt I had to leave behind. I mourned for the loss of hope I once breathed. Every moment I was in the temple that day was exactly where I needed to be...and yet, it was as if all the hard work I had done to heal had vanished.

My sister, sitting next to me, held my hand as I sobbed for two straight hours. I didn't embarrass her, and she didn't seem disappointed in me, but she just held my hand and cried with me...as her gift of love.

A phrase kept coming into my mind that day: "You still have the gift to draw from this world a garden of beauty." It was a sentence from my patriarchal blessing, which I had never paid much attention to until that day as I sat...sobbing in the temple. I had a gift to find beauty in this world? I had never read that sentence with much thought as to how it could ever be meaningful in my life. While studying my patriarchal blessing, I had skimmed over it many times, not realizing the true power it held. I had a GIFT—a spiritual gift—to find beauty in this world. At a time in my life when the world seemed so dark and ugly, I wasn't certain the phrase still applied to me, but as the years have passed, I have learned that that gift was not just a blessing...it was a driving force that helped pull me out of the darkness and into the light and beauty that still surrounded me.

Gifts. Where do they come from? What do they mean?

I will never forget the gift box of love my children made to send to families in Japan right after Emmett died. I will never forget the messages on their cards. I know that their love that day—for people they didn't even know —was because of the examples they had seen all around them. There were many times a knock came on our door from a total stranger who came bearing gifts. Countless UPS trucks stopped at our house to deliver little tokens of love. Complete strangers sent us gifts of money. I know these examples of Christ-like love impacted my children. They felt lifted because of these gifts.

I have watched tangible gifts bring much love...but I have also felt how intangible, unseen gifts bring us light. I believe that each one of us on earth was sent here with a spiritual gift or gifts... given to us by our Heavenly Father to help us lift others and fulfill our missions here on earth.

My sister Abbey has the gift of music. When she sang that song in the car as we drove to the temple, her beauty shone brightly through her voice. Ever since she was a little girl, her gift of music has brought joy to anyone who hears her. That song was a gift to me that day. My sister has always been a gift from God, but she was especially so in that moment. My mother has a gift to comfort and give spiritual advice. I have always known that about her, but I saw it even more that day as she stepped in to comfort my grieving son so that I could go find peace for myself. She too, had been seeking solace in the temple that day, and yet she sacrificed her desires for Teage and me.

Gifts are given to us all. Some come to this earth with the gift to heal. These people find themselves in callings or professions where they can heal others both mentally and physically. Doctors and medical staff spend their days using their gifts to heal the physical needs of their patients. I have a brother, Bryan, whom I text almost monthly for the answer to some sort of medical question. He has a gift to know what advice to give me about broken arms and bumps on the head. My father is a chiropractor whose healing gift has helped thousands of people find relief from the physical ailments that have held them back in the past. He has also helped me through many of the pains with which I have struggled.

Some people have the gift to help heal others emotionally or spiritually. My bishop has played a great role in helping me with his spiritual strength with which he was blessed. His gifts have come to him through his calling. I have been given great spiritual and emotional advice from many friends and family members who have shared their insights and knowledge. My brother Jeff gave me a priesthood blessing just weeks before Emmett died, which I will never forget.

After Emmett's funeral, my body was so stressed that I could no longer produce enough milk to nurse Tytus. I had to start giving him a bottle, and he started developing allergic reactions to every kind of formula we tried. He had rashes all over his skin and he couldn't keep down any food. I tried everything the doctors—or anyone else—suggested. No one seemed to have the right answer for him. For weeks, he suffered and screamed. I was becoming frantic that he would never find relief from his stomach and skin problems.

At the time I most needed help for him, the answer came in the form of a friend of mine named Jennece. She was inspired to help me find answers for my baby boy. She took time to share her many spiritual gifts with me... as she prayed for inspiration about Tytus. She has been a great source of spiritual strength for me and my kids to help us through much of the emotional pain that has held us back both mentally and physically. Her business to heal has benefited us abundantly... and my appointments and conversations with her always help me feel closer to our Heavenly Father, who blessed her with the gift of wisdom, which she shares with others.

Some people will be given the gift of friendship. A little more than a year after Emmett died, we moved into a new house. I was going through some really dark days, and my new neighbor, Noelle, was always there when I needed her. She had no idea of how hard that move was for me, but she would show up at one of my dark moments with dinner, and then, for hours, she would help me unpack. Instead of crying... I would spend the night laughing and talking with Noelle.

I have always had neighbors and friends who have generously shared their gifts with me. Ali's gift is to help look for the positive in life... and to give me something deep to think or talk about. Auna's gift is to always know when to bring dinner and just to be there to lend a listening ear. Sheryl's gift is a green thumb, which she generously shares with others. Countless times, she has brightened my day with a gift of peaches, raspberries or some other produce from her garden. Julia's gift has been to organize and create beauty out of the chaos in my closets. Cara and Krissy have the gift to get me out of the house for late-night walks. Britney's gift was to help me find clothes to wear to Emmett's funeral...and then to compulsively rearrange my house. Kiersten showed up with a new decorative piece to brighten my home. Diane's gift is the ability to make me laugh. Josh's gift has been to bring over pizza and a movie and play with my kids. Bergen comes to talk with me and make me laugh...or bring me something she has sewn—just for me. Amber showed up one day with a necklace with charms representing each one of my children, and then spent time with me just talking about life. Sunny's gift was to show up when I felt all alone during the trial. She always came with snacks and jokes to lift me up while we waited long hours at the courthouse. Tiffanie's selflessness was to sacrifice her summer and come with love to live with me, and to love me—and my children—even when I didn't always know how to show that love back for her.

I could go on all day about the gifts of friendship and love that have blessed my life. And those I have listed here don't even begin to scratch the surface of the gifts I have received from the people all around me. Each person who has touched my life has brought gifts that have enriched me. Some have physically blessed me, while others have lifted me spiritually and emotionally.

I see many who have the gift of peace. They literally bring a feeling of peace when they enter a room, and they bring peace in everything they say. I see others who have the gift of patience. When most of us would just walk away and give up, these individuals have the gift to endure to the end. I have come to know many people who possess the gift of unconditional love. Some have the gift of integrity and honesty...others, the gift of forgiveness...virtue...hope...dance...kindness...virtue. In those who have helped me along my difficult journey, I have witnessed the gift to teach...the gift to uplift...the gift of laughter...the gift of giving...the gift of moving forward...and the gift of calmness.

As a baby, Tytus, had the gift of a soft, calming spirit. People would hold him and feel the love of God radiating from him. I still see it every time he sings the LDS Primary song, *I am a Child of God*. Kaleeya has been blessed with the gift of enthusiasm. She is excited about life! She always has a dance or a song for everyone she meets. Teage has the gift of being a friend. He reminds me of Emmett in his ability to love others. He always knows just what to say to make someone feel like he or she is the most important person in the world! Bostyn has been blessed with the gift of creativity. She is an artist and has the ability to create beautiful works of art, as well as songs and dances. She has also always been able to create a lot of fun for everyone around her. Bailey has been blessed with the gift of discernment and loyalty. She is very sensitive to darkness and can sense a person's character. She is a cautious soul, and she doesn't let everyone in as a trusted friend...but if you *are* in, she is a loyal friend who will never let you go.

Emmett had the gift of openness. He always shared personal experiences and was willing to give advice. In fact, he was always so open that sometimes, it embarrassed me. He would share very intimate parts of our lives if he could see that it would make a difference for someone in their struggles. So, it doesn't surprise me that through inspiration, he asked me to continue sharing his and my very personal experiences for others to use, so they can grow and learn from our painful story.

Before coming to earth, each of our Father's spirit sons and daughters was blessed with gifts. Some of us were given many... and some of us were just given a few. No matter how many gifts you have, they will bring you and others joy. There are even more gifts you have that you may not be aware of, and it is your responsibility to find them, for they have a power for good. When you learn of a gift that Heavenly Father has blessed you with...you will find strength to polish and perfect that gift, and it will become even more powerful and refined as you use it to bless the lives of others.

I am grateful for all the gifts of others that have blessed *my* life. Each one is unique and special. But good gifts all come from a loving Father in Heaven. Some of us haven't even tapped into the gifts we have been given. I think we all have more spiritual power and strength then we can even comprehend. Pray for the light to be directed to find the gifts you hold inside, so that you can uplift others, and bring them to Christ. When they find Him through your gifts... it will be a blessing for you as well.

Even when you feel like you don't have any spiritual gifts... don't wait to dig deep to find them. I *always* had the gift to find beauty in this dark world, but I didn't comprehend the power that gift would be for my family... until the darkness had engulfed us. *All* of us are born with gifts... and all of us have the ability to find them. Search inside yourself to find out what they are. Look for them in the people around you. Pray to see what good you can find in all of your relationships. Pray for guidance to be led to the good gifts and abilities you have inside of you.

Don't let your gifts grow dim. Shine them and allow them to bless the lives of everyone around you... everyone waiting to feel your love. Don't let Satan make you doubt your abilities or talents. He wants you to hide them from the world... allowing your own selfishness to take their place. Don't do it! The minute you deprive others of your gifts... and darkness surrounds you... you risk losing them forever. Every good thing that has come my way... has been a gift from God, and most have come through the spiritual gifts of others. God doesn't come and touch our pain with His own finger. He sends blessed hands here on earth to be the hands that carry those things that brighten our days. He sends us the shoulders of others, for us to lean upon, and cry on. He sees the potential in each of us. Our only limitations are of our own choosing. The greatest gift He gave to any of us... is the gift that we can share with others.

Cherish the gifts you have right now. Live in the moment with the little blessings you've been given. Let the gift of music sing to your heart. Smile for the gift of photography... so that one day, when all you have left are memories... you will find joy from that gift. Cultivate your gifts so they will never be taken from you.

"Let your light so shine before men, that they may see your good works, and glorify your Father which is in Heaven." (*King James Bible: Matthew 5:16*).

When all is said and done, the ultimate gift He gives to us…is the gift of Eternal life…that we may live forever. Take these gifts you have received, and make forever count.

CHAPTER TWENTY-FOUR

Something is Wrong

THE DETECTIVES INVESTIGATING EMMETT'S MURDER HAD put items from his office they no longer needed into a giant plastic box. I put the box in my garage, afraid to throw anything away... I just knew that something in that box had to be evidence. Sometimes I would go out there in the middle of the night looking for clues... looking for something they had missed. I would rummage through all the paperwork, reading every bank statement, every chicken scratch on every sticky note. When I found receipts for purchases at the mall or restaurant bills, I created stories in my mind about what might have happened on that particular day. To me, everything had to be a clue, but a clue to what? That was the problem: I didn't know the answer to that question. But something was wrong!

I just felt that I was missing something, and I couldn't wait around for the trial for answers. I had to dig deeper for myself. I spent hours out there pretending that it was my job to find answers for the detectives... to do their job for them. I guess realistically, I knew I wouldn't find what they needed, but I still searched for something... that *I* needed. Maybe by chance, I would find the missing family portrait. Maybe I would find a hidden letter he had written to me telling me how much he loved me. I hoped to find correspondence between the two of them... maybe Emmett telling her he wanted out because he already had a wife whom he loved. I don't really know for sure what I was searching for—because I never did find it—but I sure knew how to waste a lot of time trying.

One of those weak moments came in the middle of the day... an urge that something was wrong pushing me to go and search through the box for clues. The little ones were napping. It must have been a Saturday because everyone was home. I took the three older kids out into the garage and told them they could play, but that I had some 'work' to do. As I searched my box, they began to wander out of the garage over to where some neighbor kids were playing. I was actually proud of them for leaving my side, and I enjoyed searching for my 'prize'—all alone—in that box full of emptiness. This time, I was convinced I would find the missing piece to the case.

Soon, I found a file with some bank statements I hadn't seen before. I began to scan through the dates and places where our credit cards had been used, trying to picture where I had been on the days in question. I turned the page over to skim through the other side. February 14th... Valentine's Day. *Victoria's Secret.* A hotel. A fancy restaurant.

My heart dropped. We hadn't spent any time together that day. No, on that Valentine's Day—just a few months earlier—I had been at home with the kids... waiting for my husband. I remember having wondered that day why Emmett's work was more important to him than me. Valentine's Day was not that big of a deal to me... but oh how I had hoped to see him walk in the door with some flowers and kisses to let me know that he loved me. He hadn't... and at the time, I had soothed my loneliness by helping the twins make elaborate Valentine's boxes for their cards. We had spent the holiday without him, but apparently, all those things he should have done for his wife, he had spent the time doing... for her.

My blood was boiling. How could he have done that to me... when I was at home taking care of our babies, with Tytus less than a month old? I read through the purchases he made that day—over and over. Each time I glanced back at the date, my heart thumped out of my chest, as if that day were happening all over again, right then.

All of the sudden, I heard Bostyn screaming. It sounded like she had been hurt. I dropped the file back into the box and ran towards the sound of the cries, but she came running to me first. She grabbed my hand and pulled me back into the garage. "Something is wrong," she cried. "Why are guns real? Why, Mom? Why is this world so bad?…Why do we have to do this? I hate that we have to live here. Why are guns real…why does this world not care about anyone? Nobody cares…why are guns even real! SOMETHING IS WRONG!"

She had no idea about what I had just read in her father's files and how badly, at that same moment, I hated the world as well. I stumbled for the words to say to her. "Bostyn, I…don't…what happened?" She threw her hands over her face and started screaming. "Those kids out there are playing with guns and one of them shot the other one. Why did Heavenly Father make guns at all? Why can't everyone just go away? They don't understand that guns will ruin them. They think this is fun. I wish we could just never do this…I never want to play ever again…something is wrong."

I wasn't sure how to comfort my daughter. Nothing was really wrong; it was just a couple of kids playing with some toys. I looked out to the street where innocent children were laughing and chasing each other. I glanced over at my box…it was just a box full of garbage and some law books. If I told her "nothing was wrong" it would be hypocritical. After all, just look at *me*; with my box full of crap…pretending I was finding answers to what was wrong…in that moment.

No matter what I found in that box, nothing was going to change for me. No matter how many times I poured through the information in that box…I was still going to be right where I was. Nothing NEW was wrong. But it felt like it. Just like my little girl sitting there blaming her tears on the events of that day, I too was taking the horrible events of the past and transforming them into brand new horrible events in the present.

A few days before Emmett died, I sat in a counselor's office for the first time, pouring out my heart to him…begging him to fix me. "I just have trust issues," I told him. "I just need you to fix me. I just need to believe in things and not question them. I am here so you can fix all the issues from my past…and help me stop feeling so scared all the time. So if you can just let me know what I need to do to fix myself, I will do anything. I have a husband whom I love more than anything! He insists that everything is great. WE are great…and so if you can just tell me how to trust…I will do whatever you think I need to do. This is how I can save my family…I have to let go of my trust issues from the past!"

The counselor sat and mostly listened to me that day. He listened to all the fears I had been bottling up inside myself. I told him of the loneliness I had been feeling. I felt as if I had been pushed away by my husband. I told him I was worried that Emmett didn't love the children or me anymore, and that something felt wrong. He sat there, quietly. I could tell he was listening with his heart.

Finally, at the end of my begging him to fix my trust issues he said, "Ashlee…you know those feelings that come from way deep down… those times when you feel like something is very wrong…" I cut him off. "Yeah, those…those are the feelings I need you to FIX," I said. "Ashlee," he continued, "those…those feelings are there for a reason. Maybe you were hurt in your past, maybe you are afraid to be hurt now…but those deep feelings inside of you…are there to keep you safe. In marriage, and in any relationship, you have to work through those feelings together. It is the job of each partner in a marriage to really take a step back and look at how to support each other through those fears…as irrational as they may seem! Every single person on this earth has insecurities and fears. Sometimes they are because of our past, but other times, they are there for an immediate reason. So each person in a relationship has the role of helping the other person find safety, through trust, love and respect. The things you are telling me today…I really believe you are right. It sounds to me like those feelings are there for a reason."

That answer gave me hope that I wasn't totally crazy, but it also left me stirring in my fear. If those feelings were there for a reason…then maybe something really *was* wrong, and how could I find answers to that? I had begged for help—from him and from others—but no one seemed to know how to quiet my fears.

A few weeks before Emmett was killed, my friend Emily stopped by to spend the day with me. It was one of those days when sheer panic had stopped me in my tracks. She finally asked me what was wrong, and it was as if she had turned on a faucet! I told her about all that was going on. I opened up to her—for the very first time— about how frightened I was that I was losing my husband. I told her about all the clues that led me to believe that something was seriously wrong.

She said, "Well, let's go follow him. Let's go find out what's going on." At the time, a part of me had thought about doing that very thing...like removing a band aid...just rip out the truth and find out for myself, and quit waiting around for him to tell me. I knew that following him might lead to answers that could be very hard to accept. It was like my heart longed for some reassurance that I wasn't crazy, but my mind knew that 'curing my crazies' might mean facing some very harsh realities.

Maybe Emily and I *should* have followed him, and found out right then what was going on, but I was afraid to see it...I was afraid to feel it. I was afraid that if I *did* find out what was really wrong, our blaming it all on my 'trust issues' wouldn't hold us together any longer. So I just sat there and did nothing...allowing the "something is wrong feeling" to just fester inside of me.

I remember the first time in my life when I got that "something is wrong" feeling. I was in third grade and my best friend lived just a few blocks away. We had permission that day to walk over to her house. As we approached her doorstep, I could hear crazy screaming and yelling inside. My friend looked so scared. She whipped her head around to me and said, "Hey...uh...my mom has probably been drinking. Wait here, and I'll be right back."

I waited outside, but I could hear everything. Her mother was screaming at everyone, and then I could tell she had started beating my friend. I could hear her begging her mother to stop...but she didn't. She hit her a lot. I was nauseous as I listened...but I did nothing. I just sat down near the side of their house, literally scared out of my mind, crying my eyes out.

Something was wrong...and there was nothing that I, a little seven-year-old girl, could do about it. Until then, I had not realized that the world could be mean. My only experiences up to that point in my life had been all about pretty things and kind words. That was the day I learned about fear. I learned that day that there will be moments when everything inside of you tells you "something is wrong!"

Later that same year, I was walking home from school with a friend. As we turned a corner, a little, white car pulled up along side of us. There were two older men in the car. The man in the passenger seat said, "Hey we need some help...we need you to get in our car and come help us find where our friend lives." He grabbed onto my arm.

Something was wrong! I could feel it. Everything inside of me told me to run. I screamed, "Run...RUN!" I ripped my hand out of his grip and my friend and I took off and ran around another corner. We hid behind a huge bush before the men had time to catch up to us. We stayed behind that bush for some time...silently breathing in deep breaths, watching the car drive past us, over and over again.

That little, white car must have passed that bush about six times before the scary feeling finally left and I knew it was safe to head home. Later, as the police sat in my driveway and asked us questions about the car and men...I felt frozen in fear. I learned more bad things about the world—that it didn't care, and that there were real-life bad guys!

Trust issues. Pain from the past. Fear. We all have them. We all need them to some degree...to keep us safe in situations when the spirit tells us to run. But then at other times, we all need our insecurities to be calmed and to go away so that we can continue on and live through our past pain. It is our job, in any relationship, to be loving, and to be respectful of the fears others might have. If someone you know and love comes to you with a concern, or tells you that something feels wrong...listen.

I had seen things go wrong in the world, I had felt the urgency to "get out" in an emergency. But with Emmett, I sat there for months silently suffering...not knowing how to let those subtle urges move me to action, blaming my fears from the past from allowing me to move forward. It wasn't because my parents got divorced the summer after I had learned—outside my friend's front door—that there was darkness in the world. It wasn't because I had dated a bunch of jerks when I was younger. It was because my marriage was broken...and I didn't even know it, until it was gone.

And then, I had to find the answers to my insecurities all by myself. My husband wasn't there to stroke my back and tell me that everything would be all right. He wasn't there to hold my hand as I learned to trust again. Emmett was dead...and somewhere inside of me...I was still searching for answers...searching for clues, searching for signs in my garage. I was pretending that finding the answers now, would somehow make everything better.

I believe there is a gift given to each of us to help us discern right from wrong. It is the Gift of the Holy Ghost. Just as there is a force in this world that tries to bring us to darkness, there is also a power of light, and I have felt the power of the Holy Ghost lead me to that light. The Holy Ghost has been for me what a Disney movie describes as our 'conscience.' The Holy Ghost works as our constant guide: those silent whisperings in our hearts when something is not quite right. There are moments that stop us in our tracks, when something much greater than ourselves is trying to reach us. I believe these gentle urges come from the Holy Ghost.

When my twins were babies, I remember a day when I had just tucked them into their beds for a nap. I shut their door and began walking down the stairs. Halfway down the stairs, I got an overwhelming impression to go back up and check on them. At first I thought, *No...they are fine. I was just in there.*

But something kept telling me to turn around and go back in their room to make sure they were okay. I opened the door and heard the weirdest sound coming from Bostyn's crib. Somehow, she had rolled over and her blanket had wrapped around her head. She was gasping for air, but the blanket over her face was hindering her attempts to breathe. I quickly unwrapped her, and she took a giant breath.

I *know* I was prompted that day on those stairs. I hardly ever went back to check on the twins during their naps...because the door would squeak and wake them up. A power much greater than my own instincts had told me that something was wrong...and it was...and I did something about it.

Sometimes we are quietly searching alone in the darkness of our garages...for answers to our problems, trying to grasp onto anything to help our lives make sense. Wasting hours on nothing. I was so afraid not to know everything Emmett had done...but I was even more afraid of the answers I was searching for all by myself. On those days, I didn't ask for professional help...and I certainly didn't seek guidance from the Lord. Absorbed by complete self-pity...I did it all alone.

You don't have to search alone. Ask for the Holy Ghost to be your companion as you search for what is wrong. He will guide you. And in those moments when you need to stop searching and just look within yourself...He will comfort you. He will send you the still, small voice to lead you to what is important. He knows you are searching alone... but if you search for Christ, instead, His voice will guide you to the light that only He can bring. Don't spend your hours searching for clues in the dark. Use His love to light your path. Use His peace to still your soul. Allow His spirit to guide you in your search when you feel that something is wrong. And when you are confused about whether you are suffering because of past hurts, or whether there is something happening right now, His spirit will enlighten you...and give you peace.

Bostyn had those fears for a reason...but the reason wasn't in that moment. It was from something that had happened in her past. *I was looking for clues about past hurts in a box...not because it would change anything for me, but because my fears of the past still motivated me to seek peace.* It hadn't helped to have others tell me I was crazy, but if I had been able to find the love I was searching for, it would have changed me. If Emmett had been there for me in my moments of fear...a lot of things would have been different.

Bostyn didn't need me to tell her that she was crazy. It was my job as her mother to comfort her and help calm her fears. She didn't need to hear how over-dramatic she was being. She needed to find peace in a moment when everything inside of her was telling her "something was wrong".

We all have insecurities. We all have fears that drive us to question... ourselves...our doubts...even the truth. It is easy in life to get mixed up about what is an unfounded doubt and what is a truth. Let the Holy Ghost guide you...and help you determine if those fears are there because something really *is* wrong, or because something was wrong in the past, and you haven't been able to let it go.

What people in your life are begging for your patience and love as they work through their insecurities? How many times have you just told them to stop being so paranoid...to blindly trust? Maybe it isn't a lack of trust in you, maybe those insecurities are there because they are failing to see how to let go of their past. How have they felt when you squelched their fear instead of acknowledging it through your trust and love? We have a responsibility to be there for those around us who are afraid. Yes, maybe their fears are not because of anything we did or didn't do...maybe their feelings that something is wrong come from their lives before we knew them, or a part of their past of which we were not a part, but it doesn't change the fact that the fears driving them...feel so real.

Before he died, Emmett had spent months telling me I was just hallucinating...that I was crazy. I remember a few times I would run out to his car as he was driving away for work. He would roll down his window to say goodbye. With tears in my eyes I would ask "Is everything okay... I feel scared, what is happening?...I need your help." He would get frustrated with me and tell me to stop being so paranoid. As he would drive away, I would just stand there feeling completely empty inside. The fear in my heart felt more than just my past pains creeping in...*something* felt very wrong.

In my case, something *had* been wrong....I *wasn't* crazy! I remember when the detectives shut the front door that night after telling me about Emmett's death, as I sat there with my sister Ali and her boyfriend, Will, my first reaction was to hit the couch and scream, "I told you I wasn't crazy!" Screaming and punching... relieved that I wasn't crazy... punching my hand into the cushion, letting that cushion know I had been right! I punched the couch for all the times I had opened up and no one could help me. I punched it for all the clues that had been leading me to the answers I had been seeking, but mainly, I abused that cushion for all the important people to whom I had pled for help who told me that I just needed to "get over it... because this is real life!"

Something *had been* wrong, but nobody, not even me, had known what to do about it. I was humiliated that I found out the truth on the same night everyone else did. Yes, I was scared because Emmett was gone....I was devastated that he had been murdered... and furious that he had been unfaithful to me... but my very first emotion was a sense of relief that I finally had an answer to my impression that 'something was wrong!'

I will never fully understand how shock works. In my case, it was as if it shut off my ability to choose which emotions came over me. The first emotion that came for me—as crazy as it sounds—was relief... relief that all my feelings that something was wrong... were real. I *wasn't* crazy. That feeling of relief... it scared the hell out of me. I felt like a horrible person. Out of all the emotions I should have been feeling in that moment...I was relieved that those impressions that had been churning inside me and eating me alive...had been there for a reason. My heart had been right. I *wasn't* feeling those things because I was broken from my past. The counselor had been correct...but unfortunately, now it was too late. My sense of relief was brief...but when it hit, it felt so good to know my instincts had been right. It wasn't just because I had trust issues...it was because the Holy Ghost had been whispering to me and impressing upon my mind that something was wrong.

Understand that your spouse needs to feel that he or she is the most important person to you. Cherish that relationship. If you have any other relationships—a coworker, an old high school friend, another parent in your kid's class—that make your spouse feel uncomfortable, no matter how irrational it may seem to you, PLEASE put your spouse first, the person who matters most in your life. Don't fight over relationships that aren't worth fighting for. Comfort the fears of those people who truly matter in your life. Eventually, after they see that they come first no matter what, their fears will be calmed...but work together until they do. It is not your job to bring others happiness. That is a choice they have to make for themselves...but sometimes their fears...might actually protect you from unbearable heartache...if you will just listen.

Emmett thought I was just being insecure when I shared with him the feelings I had the minute I heard Kandi's name. But my fears were right. Em and I were a team...but in that moment...he ignored my fears, and placed his desires above our partnership...and eventually, our team was shattered.

There will be moments when a feeling will come into your mind... telling you that something isn't right. Yes, sometimes it is something we need to let go of from the past...but when it is deep down...insisting that something is really wrong...don't let it go. It may be there for a reason. It may be there trying to lead you. It may be there for you to open up a lie that is hiding. Don't wait until all you have left are the clues in a dark garage in a box full of dead ends. Whatever that moment is for you ... ask for love as you find answers. Seek for guidance until you find peace. Don't wait until it is too late, and as in my case, have the answers come to you at the same moment they are told to the rest of the world. Follow the still small voice. ... It is a voice of warning. It is a voice of comfort. It is a voice of guidance in all the roads you travel. And its power can be a voice of truth to you in the moments when something *is* wrong.

CHAPTER TWENTY-FIVE

Voices

AT THE BEGINNING OF APRIL, AFTER EMMETT'S death, it
was time for LDS General Conference. We had always made Conference
weekends special when I was a kid, and Emmett and I had carried on the
tradition. We would sit as a family, listening to every talk...snuggled on
the couch with our favorite treats and snacks.

I felt uneasy about just sitting around our house and watching it this
year. My mom, who was still staying with us, suggested we call my Aunt
Diane—who lived just two hours away—to see if we could go and spend
the weekend with her. Rob had just been bailed out of jail, so I really felt
the need to get away for a while. We decided to go to Diane's. All of us
needed to get out of the house, and I looked forward to some time away
to think, and not do anything but listen to the counsel and direction from
the leaders of the Church.

As we drove away from the house, it almost felt as if a weight had been
lifted off my back. I looked out over the valley. It looked so dark and grey.
It felt nice to leave the heaviness of our reality, and drive towards a place
where so many people loved us. The kids were calm in the car. Everyone
seemed to be lapping up the peace that seemed to have enveloped the car.
It felt good to have some time to just think and be...not worrying about
life, or death, or anything, really. My mind felt at peace.

As we pulled into Diane's driveway, my phone rang. It was an uniden-
tified number, which usually meant a detective or an attorney on the case.

I stayed in the car to answer the phone while my mother unloaded the kids. I sat watching my family joyfully run in and give kisses to everyone. The call was from the victim's witness coordinator with the Attorney General's Office. She was calling to tell me about the upcoming hearing dates, information about Rob, and to update me on everything the office had been working on.

At the end of our conversation she said, "So, we were all wondering, do you want to be involved?...Do you want to come to these hearings?... Do you want us to reserve a spot for you, or do you just want us to call you after each hearing and give you an update so you don't have to sit through them?" I didn't reply immediately. I just sat there for a minute... unsure about what I really did want. What should I do? "Well, I guess..." I began. "I'm not really sure...what do you recommend to someone in my position...what do people usually do? What do you tell everyone else to do?"

She was silent for a minute. "Ashlee...you know...I don't know that we've ever had anyone who has been in your position before, so this is one of those cases...where I can't really tell you what people usually do, because... well, I've never really known anyone who has been where you are right now."

I hung up the phone. I felt paralyzed. I felt alone. I know she was just trying to help me realize that I would have to make my own decision, but in that moment, her words spoke to my insecurities and doubts. I really *was* alone. There was no one else who had ever been exactly where I was. It was just me. I felt cold...almost bitter. I had no one to call for advice. They couldn't refer me to the last woman who had walked in my shoes. I was not the norm. Despite all my desires to just have a normal life—the life I had always craved—I was the exception. There was no one who had ever been in my same situation.

My excitement to listen to Conference faded as I picked up my bag and carried it inside. The weight that had been briefly lifted as we had driven away from home, fell once again onto my back. I was all alone. I felt like none of the talks that weekend would be for me. No, they would be for all the *perfect* husbands and wives. They would be for all the *perfect* parents raising *perfect* children. I started to feel like Conference wouldn't be for me this year. That fear wouldn't prevent me from listening, but nonetheless, I was certain I would be disappointed. Nobody knew what my pain felt like...and nobody had ever been where I had been.

When Saturday morning came, I still had a pit in my stomach. I wasn't excited about Conference the way I had always been in the past. I sat through the first three or four talks almost purposefully refusing to allow anything to penetrate the wall I had erected around myself. I stared out toward the TV...but I didn't hear a word. I was completely focused inward, feeling sorry for myself—no one had ever been through what I had suffered, or had felt the type of pain that was my constant companion.

Another talk began, and I folded my arms...perhaps an unconscious sign of self-pity. Then, I prayed to God for a miracle...that I could hear something that would speak to my frozen heart. I pled with Him to lift the black hole surrounding me so I could feel light again. Even though I knew that none of the speakers had ever walked in my shoes, I begged God to inspire one of them to let me know that I was not alone.

All of the sudden . . . my ears started working, and for the first time that day, I listened to the words being spoken and the principles being taught. The speaker, Elder Kent F. Richards of the Seventy, spoke of pain, and as his words filled the room, I felt in my heart that the pain I felt that day had not been forgotten. (*The Atonement Covers All Pain*. LDS General Conference April 2011).

His message was clear. For the first time since Emmett died I had an inspired witness that I was not alone. Maybe nobody had been in my situation... maybe I didn't have a friend to call for advice about how involved I should be in the murder trial, or how best to move forward to find peace ...maybe I had no one to pave the way along my pathway to healing...

maybe I was alone in my battle, but as my ears finally opened, and my emotions came pouring out as I listened to that message sent to me... from God, I knew He wasn't very far away. He knew I would have pain. He knew I would be asked to make grown-up decisions—which I felt far too young to make—but He wasn't asking me to make them without Him. He wanted me to know that, because He needed me to live like I believed every word.Maybe nobody had been in my situation... maybe I didn't have a friend to call for advice about how involved I should be in the murder trial, or how best to move forward to find peace... maybe I had no one to pave the way along my pathway to healing... maybe I was alone in my battle, but as my ears finally opened, and my emotions came pouring out as I listened to that message sent to me... from God, I knew He wasn't very far away. He knew I would have pain. He knew I would be asked to make grown-up decisions—which I felt far too young to make— but He wasn't asking me to make them without Him. He wanted me to know that, because He needed me to live like I believed every word.

I could *feel* every single talk after that. I knew the words being taught were not just for all the "perfect couples" surrounding me... they were for me, too. The next talk was about women and the strength they possess. At the end, the speaker thanked all those single women struggling to work things out on their own. In another talk after that, the speaker assured me that God "knows you and He sees your sacrifice..."

In the afternoon session, there was a talk about a man who lost his wife because the doctor who came to help her deliver her baby transmitted an illness to her from an earlier patient. She died a few days later. Her husband was bitter and wanted to ruin that doctor's life. He was told by a Church leader to "leave it alone." Later in his life, he came to understand the wisdom of having followed that advice. He realized he would have ruined his own life—and the life of the doctor—had he not followed the counsel to "Leave it alone." In each talk, there was a little bit of something I needed to hear.

There are voices all around us... telling us how we should feel... and who *they* think we should be. During this difficult time of my life, I heard many voices that tried to bring me down. Some tried to belittle me. Opinions were freely shared about how I should be feeling. People told me I should be moving on... or how to grieve. Some told me I should be moving on more quickly, while others said I should slow down. None of those voices really mattered. Heavenly Father knew what path I needed to take on my journey, and only He had the true answers for my particular situation.

I was alone that day in my own personal grief... but I was not forgotten. Every single person has their own story. Every one of us has our own personal path of pain. Not one of us has a handbook that details what comes next or how we should handle or make decisions. What is right for one... might be totally wrong for another. However, I have never been led astray when I have followed the counsel of the Prophets. Their counsel should be our handbook. They speak to us with no agenda. They volunteer their lives to speak truths to us. They care about each of us and about our relationships. They care about how we are living our lives and handling our grief.

During the trial, I had some special visitors ask to come to my home one Sunday afternoon to spend some time with me and my family. These men, who work alongside the Prophet daily, were there in my living room to see if I was okay. One of the first things they said was, "President Monson has asked that we come to see how you are doing... and to let you know that we have been praying for you."

They didn't have an agenda... they didn't come to get the gossip. They came to show me that I wasn't alone. They were sent by the leader of the Church to remind me that I wasn't alone... and I knew it was true. I didn't know it because of them, I knew it was true because I felt it in my heart. Heavenly Father's spirit was so strong. They came to comfort me and help me REMEMBER that He was not very far away... He knew right where I was... and I was not alone.

I know the words spoken by our Church leaders are true. I know that when I listen to all they teach me, I can feel joy here on earth. I believe that when we follow their teachings, we can remain immovable and true to our faith, even when the pains of this world are more than we can bear on our own.

We are all going to get knocked down. It's not about getting knocked down...it's about what we do when we get back up. Whatever pain has brought *you* down, find a way to get to your knees...and while you are there, pray for the courage to one day learn how to stand again. It may take years to let it all go. It may take a lifetime to find peace. It may take a thousand prayers to find relief from your pain. All pains in life are covered by a loving Father in Heaven who knows how to heal you. Some pains might take time to heal, some might never leave you while you are on this earth... but even through your pain you can find joy...if you have faith in Him.

The world will tell us that we are not enough. People will make us feel like we are not measuring up in any of the things we do. And most of the time, we listen. We allow the world to tell us that being a "stay at home mom" is not a worthy title. The world will whisper to us that our potential is so much more than just sitting home changing diapers. Voices are everywhere...in every magazine we read, in every commercial we watch. Voices. Speaking to us. Make sure the voices *you* hear are the ones speaking words that are worthy of your time. Don't let the world's whisperings pull you away from the pathway to true happiness.

All of us walk our own roads. No one has ever been exactly where you are. In this moment right now...no one else has felt what you are feeling. That fact can feel overwhelmingly lonely and hard. It is a truth that sometimes leaves you wondering where to turn and what to do next. During those moments when you feel like you have no one to call, and no one to tell you who to be...just be YOU. You are the you that He wanted you to be. He has the power to heal the you He still sees inside. And He will. He is the one who has walked your path ahead of you. He has seen the darkness. He has felt the hurt. He walks a few steps ahead, so He is prepared to find a way to wipe the tears from your eyes, and mend the holes in your heart.

You were made to be you. If you are going to disappoint anyone, let it be those who cannot find the goodness inside of you…the ones who look for all that is wrong with you. They will bombard you until you lose sight of yourself. Voices are everywhere. Listen carefully. Listen to the ones that lift you up. Surround yourself with beauty… and as you do, you will find your own voice. Listen to the voices that help you stand.

CHAPTER TWENTY-SIX

For Good

ONE DAY, MY FRIEND BERGEN WAS AT my house chatting with me and said, "You know, you should really hire someone to come stay with you for the summer to help you when you have meetings and counseling appointments, and everything else you have going on. What about your cousin Tiffanie... she would be the perfect person for the job."

My first thought was of what Tiffanie had done just the year before. She had spent the entire summer helping my Grandma, whose husband had just passed away. Tiffanie had already spent a summer with a widow... like she would want to come do that again! But the idea felt right, so I texted her.

By that night, she and I had made plans. She would come as soon as college was out for the summer and stay until school began again in the fall. It gave me something to look forward to. I was excited to have an extra set of hands, and it would also help me to do some fun things with the kids during the upcoming summer.

The week finally came when school was out. On the day she arrived, she brought her sister Taylor and our Grandma "Berna" because they all had tickets to go see the musical *WICKED*. At the last minute, Tiffanie's mother, who was supposed to go with them, called to say she couldn't make it. She told me that I could have her ticket if I wanted it. I was excited! I knew nothing about the show. I had never even heard any of the songs, but I was happy to take her place and spend a night out with the girls.

We drove downtown to the theater. I hated going downtown, and tried to avoid it at all costs. It always brought back memories: the hospital where Tytus was born, the grocery store where we'd stopped while I was in labor to get a doughnut for me before the hospital starved me. Emmett's old office. The courthouse where I knew the dreaded trial would take place. Driving past all of these places always left a pit in my stomach. On the other hand, it was nice taking the drive with other people in the car, and driving there for a purpose other than something having to do with my past.

We finally came to the Opera House and found a parking spot. We made our way into the building. I saw a few people I knew, gave some hugs, and then we found our seats. It was relaxing to be in a building where everyone seemed so excited and content. I loved the energy I felt in that hall.

Soon the music started up and the lights were dimmed. The show began. I was mesmerized. The stage was bright, and the music was enchanting. It was like every care in MY world just disappeared as I listened to the story and got lost in the melodies. Everything inside me was calm, and in that moment, I forgot all the fears and pain that awaited me when reality would once again hit at the end of the play.

The story was about two girls who were never really meant to be friends. In fact, they hated each other. They were complete opposites. As the plot moves along, they end up becoming a great team to fight the corruption they saw around them.

Toward the end of the play, the main characters, Elphaba and Galinda, come to a crossroads, knowing they might be saying goodbye to each other for the last time. The music began . . . the first words were sung . . . and my tears began to fall . . .

For Good spoke to my heart; every word in that song felt as if it was written for me. Tears fell down my cheeks, and with every note sung . . . I missed Emmett from the depths of my soul. I pictured us singing this

duet. I could almost see him begging me to continue on, despite him being gone. I pictured him pleading with me to forgive him for all the things he had done, and for all the things he had left unsaid. I felt his arms surround me as I watched those characters sing to each other on the stage. I felt his love. I felt his regret. My heart ached for all the duets we would never sing, for all the love songs we had sung together . . . that were now in the past . . . and for all the songs he left me still singing . . . without him.

I could almost hear him begging me to carry on his journey, asking me to change others through the story of his pain, letting me know that he needed me now, more than ever, to continue his mission to do good on the earth. For the first time since he died, I realized that he DID need me, and he always had. All the anger I had been carrying seemed to disappear for the duration of the song, and all the good that he had been to me was brought to my remembrance.

I wasn't sure that day if I had been changed for the better, but I knew that because I had known Emmett... I had been changed for good.

He left me at a time when I doubted the reality of our love, and when I was questioning the purpose of my pain... but that didn't mean he hadn't

changed me for the better. I couldn't understand why he was gone. I don't know that I will *ever* grasp why I had been left to find my way in this world without him...through a time when *he* was the one who held the key to healing me and answering all my doubts. I couldn't understand why *he* had to be the sacrifice for someone else's pain. I will never have the opportunity to hear him explain why he betrayed our marriage.

His choices had brought me so much heartache, and his murder had shattered my dreams...but nonetheless, he had still left me with so much for which I could still be thankful. He gave me thousands of smiles. He gave me years of joy. We had times in our marriage when he made me feel like I was on top of the world. We laughed together as we struggled through years of school. We held on to each other through miscarriages and sickness. We held hands during the funerals of many of our beloved family members. We danced at many weddings. We created so many moments of love. We were blessed with unlimited blessings. He and I had built a life that I loved...and it was all still right in front of me. He gave me five beautiful children, whom I wouldn't trade for anything. We created them together, in love. He changed me for the better, and even though he was gone...he touched my life while he was here.

Through the years, there have been many people who have changed me for good. Taylor and Grandma held my hands while I cried that night. Tiffanie would end up spending her entire summer changing me and the kids for good, being a support for us in our greatest time of need. It was more than just a summer job of changing diapers, helping children across the street, and blowing up water wings. It was the moments when she helped us to stand...when all we could do was stumble without her help. She has always been one of my best friends, but that summer...Tiffanie was my Angel.

My journey has been full of Angels...some who can be seen with my eyes, and others who I can only feel with my heart. But there hasn't been a moment when I haven't felt them near.

Sometimes people come into our lives for only a moment; sometimes they come and stay for a while. And then there are those who leave us way too soon. When they go, all we have left are the memories of how we have been changed because of them. Whoever they are, and whatever they bring...our paths cross for a reason. And, for every soul who has

touched yours, you have made a difference to them as well.

Every life is made up of a series of impacts...a list of moments when others interact with us. We cannot avoid them. Some will be blessings in our lives and others will be more like collisions that will leave us injured and damaged. Sometimes, you will be the one to impact another person. Other times, it will be someone who will impact you. It is our responsibility to make sure our impact on others will be for good. It is up to us as well, to find the faith to overcome those moments when the impact of others on us has left us broken.

Each of these moments are what create your history. Make sure you leave a legacy worth telling. Live your life as if every moment of impact you have on another person will be your last. Don't breeze through your days without taking the time to make each day count, for good.

Every soul you meet has a purpose. Everyone you shake hands with has a story. Every story is based on an individual's attempts to build positive relationships. Every moment that touches your life...has meaning. Find it. We are not put together by accident, and even when we are forced to part...it is for reasons much greater than we will ever comprehend. Sometimes, there are new roads we are being asked to travel. There are lessons in every story, morals at the end of every day. There is still good to be found.

We cannot write our stories alone. It is up to each soul we touch, and each spirit that finds ours... to write our stories together. Every person you meet will leave something for you, and you will leave behind memories for them. Each moment of impact will define who we will become. Make a difference in those moments when others are falling... and search

for strength in those moments when you must stand. Every impact... every second of your history will be part of YOUR story. Each time your life is touched, you can be changed for good.

CHAPTER TWENTY-SEVEN

Love

I REMEMBER ONE DAY BEING SO 'CHECKED out' that I hardly talked to my kids. I was frazzled and running. I was avoiding anything that had to do with real life and my reality. I don't remember what we even did that day, because my mind was so far removed. I do remember, however, that all day long the twins kept asking me to give them some time. They are the reserved, calm types and don't really demand my time like my other children do. So on that particular day, it was easy to let their tender needs be swept under the rug. I kept putting them off. Each time they asked me to come and talk with them, I was busy with the younger kids. I didn't think much of it, and I just kept doing other tasks every time they came to me.

I put all of the kids to bed without giving another thought to the fact that I hadn't taken the time to talk with my girls. I drew myself a hot bath and relaxed. It was nice to soak in the water and not think. The security alarm was on, and everyone was in bed. It was just me and the quiet. I was so out of it on this particular day that even the silence didn't threaten to stir up my emotions. I just sat there and didn't think at all.

I must have been in there for a good half-hour or more before I started to turn into a prune. I reached for my towel. As I looked up into the fogged-up mirror I could see some writing on the glass. I got closer. My heart skipped a beat. I read the words out loud, "I love you!" I stood there dripping wet, staring at those words on that mirror without taking a breath. They were words *I* had written.

My mind went back in time. A few days before Emmett died, I had written 'I love you!' on the mirror with my finger when he was in the shower, hoping that when he got out, he would see my message and feel it. I prayed with all of my heart that he would see it and that it would touch him. I don't know if he did. He never mentioned anything about it...but I doubt he could have missed it. However, it didn't change anything...or soften him.

I hated the thought that my efforts hadn't had the hoped-for results. Tears fell down my face as I stood there reviewing the events of that morning, not so long before, when I had been begging him to love me. I hadn't just written those words up on the mirror to help him feel loved. No, the message was a warning sign to him as well. I had been pleading with him as I wrote...that I needed him. I needed him to love ME.

I couldn't believe the message hadn't faded or been washed away. How was it that I hadn't seen it before? I have no idea. That night, the words of a message, which I had written with so much hope before my husband's death, took on a new meaning to me. The words were not just a reminder of all the things that hadn't changed. No, that night, I felt they were a message to me. Those words were a reminder to me that I *was* loved. Not only by Emmett, but by Heavenly Father. This time, both of them were begging ME to step outside of myself...and love.

I had to learn to love myself. I had to learn to love my babies. And one day, I had to learn to fall in love again. Love—the very emotion which had been drained from me during the weeks that followed my writing that message on the mirror—all of the sudden seemed to fill my soul.

I went into my closet and put on one of Emmett's old sweatshirts. It was a sweatshirt with good memories, which I had saved for a moment just like this. It was a navy blue hoody I had seen him wear so many times. It still smelled like him. If I closed my eyes, that scent seemed so real. I wrapped my arms around myself. It was warm and I felt so cozy being snuggled inside it. I lay down on my closet floor, dreaming of the first time I had seen Emmett wearing it...

I was working in the school gym at college. Adam, one of my co-worker's, came downstairs, winked at me, and said "I need you to bring this stack of towels up to me in five minutes." I said, "Oh dear... what are you up to, Adam?" He answered, "Well, a buddy of mine just moved up here this week and he's been talking about this girl he keeps seeing at the gym. Once we figured out it was you, I told him I would introduce you guys."

Adam drew me right in! Five minutes later, I carried the towels up the stairs, feeling just like a fifteen-year-old girl. I set them down and looked up. Over walked this navy blue sweatshirt, with the cutest thing I had ever seen wrapped inside it. I had also noticed *him* around the gym that week. In fact, just the day before, he had been running on the treadmill while I was cleaning the equipment. I couldn't help but stare at him as he ran. I finally got to the machine, next to him. It took me a good five minutes longer to clean it than the others before it. I just sat there wiping, and wondering how to start up a conversation with him. I never did think of anything good to say! Years later, we still laughed about my extensive and thorough cleaning of that treadmill... while we both tried to figure out what to say to each other.

But on that day, as I set the towels down, there was someone else there making sure we did say something to each. Emmett and I chatted for a while. We found we had a common link to Boise because both of our fathers lived there, so we talked about that and other things. I thought he was adorable.

All that week, my roommates had been begging me to find a date for a "roommate date." I hadn't found anyone I wanted to ask, so I got brave with Emmett. "Hey," I said. "So, I have a favor to ask of you. All of my roommates have made dates for a movie, and I was wondering if you would come and be my date?" He said, "Yeah, sure. When is it?" "Well," I said sheepishly, "in an hour. You want to go?"

One hour later, I picked him up. He had changed out of that navy blue sweatshirt. He cleaned up well! We went on the roommate date to the movie and then afterwards, the two of us went out to dinner. Then he took me to his apartment and we talked and listened to music for hours. He was my dream boy... and I had only known him for a few hours! I was smitten.

After that, we never spent a second apart. We were glued at the hip. Every second I was with him, I fell more and more in love with him. When he asked me to marry him around Christmastime... there was not a doubt in my mind what my answer would be. I loved him, and I wanted to start a family with him. I wanted to spend my life loving him and taking care of his babies...

As I lay there in the closet, my mind snapped out of the daydream I was having, and I remembered that my twins had begged for my love all day long, and I had completely ignored them. I ran out of my closet and bedroom, and stumbled up the stairs. Wiping the tears off my face, I cracked open their door and peeked inside. "Girls... hey... are you still awake?" Bostyn answered from her side of the room. "Hey Mom..." I tiptoed over to her, and then sat down on the edge of her bed. Then Bailey's eyes opened and she hopped out of bed and came over and sat next to me, putting her arms around me.

"Girls... I am so sorry. I was a horrible mom today. You guys asked me a million times to come and talk and I never did... and I want you to know that I am sorry. I am sorry I can't do what I should be doing lately... It's like I don't remember how to do anything.... and I know I'm not there for you... and I get more frustrated than usual with everything. I am so sorry that I..."

Bostyn cut me off. "Mom... everything is going to be okay. Bailey and I were up here crying and crying and wishing you would come up and talk to us. We felt lonely... and scared. We were getting really upset and mad at you for ignoring us all day. We didn't know what to do... and so we said a prayer. After our prayer, Daddy was standing right over there and he told us that everything is going to be okay. He said he loves us and he is proud of us all...especially you. He said he misses us and he wants us to help you learn how to love again."

That night, I cried buckets of tears...but not just for the love I had lost. I cried tears for all the love I was blessed to find. My tears were for the love I needed to remember...for all of the people who were still standing and waiting for me to love them.

Heavenly Father hears our prayers. He sends us signs to let us know He loves us. Heavenly Father loves you no matter how hard you push Him away or ignore Him. He loves you no matter how many signs you have already missed. Sometimes, He sends them in little 'I love you's' on our mirrors...and other times He sends a miracle to help us do the jobs we are failing to do.

Love is a gift we all possess. Don't hide it. Wear it proudly. Live it free-ly...and let its power guide you to all the little souls who are crying up in their rooms all alone...waiting for you...wondering how they can teach you how to love them back. Show them that you hear them. Listen the first time. My fears had stopped me in my tracks. It was as if I couldn't feel or give love to those left behind with me. Emmett wasn't here to read my messages, but my little babies still needed me to write them.

Watch for all the signs on your mirrors—flashing in your face—from those who are begging to receive your love. Listen for the tender plead-ings that they need you. They want you. Don't let the message get wiped off the mirrors before you act.

Don't be afraid when love has left mud on your face to wash it off and find a way to trust in it all over again. Take a chance, even when you don't feel like you have any space for love left inside of you. Pray for room in your heart to allow love to fill it with all the joy it can bring. Listen to all of the little reminders. You are capable of loving...you are worthy of it...and you deserve it. Sometimes, it won't come to you until you find it in yourself. Believe in the *you* that He sees. He loves you and wants you to LOVE yourself. Be true to the you inside, and learn to trust that it is enough.

In all of your relationships—no matter what they are—let love bring you closer together. Sometimes it will hurt, sometimes it will fail, and sometimes you will feel like it is gone forever. Love…and do it like you have never lost it. Don't let your fear of losing someone stop you from loving that person with all of your heart.

CHAPTER TWENTY-EIGHT

Taking the Leap

EMMETT AND I GOT HOOKED ON THE show *Parenthood*. It is about an extended family and the highs and lows of their lives. We loved all the different dynamics of the characters and how they each had such an authentic story. All of the families had their own dramas, but they worked together to get through them. We loved the reality of their stories and the different circumstances they portrayed.

One night, not long after the funeral, my sister Abbey and I decided to watch the show for the first time since Emmett's death. The episode was called *Taking the Leap*. It was not as eventful as some of the past episodes, but I remember having a pit in my stomach as we watched that day. I had seen these characters so many times, facing all sorts of situations and hardships of everyday family life. Nothing in particular about the episode connected with me, but I started bawling like a baby.

My sister turned to me, "Ash … are you okay? Do you want me to turn it off?" I replied through my sobs, almost laughing at the same time, "Remember when we used to watch this show … and I thought these people had problems? Now, I would trade places with them in a heartbeat. Their problems seem so simple now."

I had sat on this couch so many times before following the lives of these characters, being almost judgmental of the decisions they made and of how they handled their hardships. I sat on my pedestal looking down on the way they handled their stress, and I was disgusted by how they constantly messed up when they came to a crossroad. Now, I wanted to beg these people, whom I once pitied, to switch places with me! I was stuck—even more than any of them—in a situation I was struggling with, and which I hadn't chosen. I was left with a path to walk, that I had never planned on trudging. For the first time, I saw these characters for what they really were...normal families living their lives to the best of their abilities with what they had been given. They were struggling to find answers; they were striving to find joy, even when life had thrown them lemons. They were working hard to be the best parents they could be, even on the hard days. I realized that they were taking a leap, every single day. They were taking leaps of faith in all of their relationships and were striving to live the best lives they could.

After Emmett's death, Bostyn and Bailey were the first ones to have a birthday—just a little over a month after the funeral. As the day approached, I found myself dreading it. When I had been growing up, my family had never been big on birthdays. Emmett's family, on the other hand, always knew how to make birthdays special. For most of his childhood, he was an only child and his mom had always put a lot of time and energy into his birthdays. She always threw him an amazing party with a theme, and after our children were born, she and Emmett loved making their birthdays fun and full of life. This year, I simply couldn't do it alone. There wasn't much life left in me, and how could I possibly give any of my remaining energy to a birthday?

The day came. I was down and low, feeling so sorry for myself. I spent much of the morning sneaking into my closet sanctuary to shed private tears. Once again, I was in zombie mode, not sure how to celebrate without Emmett. I was overwhelmed with the thought that he was missing their birthday, and I felt even more uneasy about my ability to make it a special day for them. I had hardly planned a thing.

I have no idea where the cake came from. Before Emmett's death, I made the girls a special cake every year. When they turned one, their favorite animals were ducks, so Emmett's mother and I made the most adorable 3D duck cakes. She decked them out in beautiful gowns, and we took them to the zoo with all their little friends to feed the ducks. It was an adorable birthday celebration that I would never have been able to put together without the help of Emmett and his mom. Every birthday since then had been the same: fun, themed, and organized. It wasn't because of me. I just followed their lead and did my best to keep up.

This time, however, it was just me. I didn't know how to do it without Emmett. When it was almost time to sing...I found myself heading back to my closet again. I couldn't do this. I almost felt like I didn't deserve to watch these girls celebrate when Emmett couldn't be there. *He* was the one that always swore he would never miss a birthday...not me.

As I turned the corner to escape to my safe haven, my Aunt Diane grabbed my arm. "Hey, are you okay? Is there something I can do to help you through this today?" I fell into her arms and let out the tears I had been shedding alone. "I don't know how to do this. It's not fair. Why is he missing it? He is going to miss it all...every birthday. It's not like this will be the only one. He isn't coming back."

She held me for a minute while I sobbed. Her embrace reassured me as I thought back on all of the kids' special birthdays in the past. She whispered, "You can do this for them, Ash."

I looked back at her. I could do this? I knew she was right...I had to take a leap and live this day. I told her I would be out in a minute, and I went and sought a moment of refuge in my closet. I sat there remembering all the days we had spent singing *Happy Birthday* to our babies. I thought about all the times we sang their favorite songs. I wrestled with the anger I felt toward Emmett for leaving me alone, and the conflicting sadness that gnawed inside of me because he was going to miss it all. The words of a song kept coming to my mind. It was a song we had sung to the twins every night since the day they were born.

I looked back at her. I could do this? I knew she was right . . . I had to take a leap and live this day. I told her I would be out in a minute, and

I went and sought a moment of refuge in my closet. I sat there remembering all the days we had spent singing Happy Birthday to our babies. I thought about all the times we sang their favorite songs. I wrestled with the anger I felt toward Emmett for leaving me alone, and the conflicting sadness that gnawed inside of me because he was going to miss it all. The words of a song kept coming to my mind. It was a song we had sung to the twins every night since the day they were born.

Yes, I knew that everything in the world wasn't wonderful, but I also knew I had to force myself to find the wonder that was still there. I had to take the leap to understand that the babies I used to rock to sleep while I sang of the earth's wonder…needed me to see that they were among those wonderful parts left in the world. There *was* beauty all around me. I was failing to see that the only thing holding me back from feeling it, was myself.

Humbled, I walked out of my closet into a room full of smiles. We sang *Happy Birthday*—for the first time since Emmett had died. Each word of the song hit my soul a little harder. I stared at my babies, the girls I now had to watch grow up without a husband by my side. And they had to grow up without their father.

Their eyes never left my gaze. It was as if their souls were waiting for me to smile, to let them know that I could see them, and that I could remember they *were* wonderful. Their precious blue eyes—which always used to sparkle—seemed covered in a fog. They were smiling, but that haze wasn't going to clear up until I showed them how to make it go.

I thought of all the pain Emmett's absence brought to my heart. I could see the same pain in the eyes of everyone in the room…and yet they were still smiling. I took a leap…a tiny smile came to my face. The girls' grins became bigger as mine grew. Almost instantly, I saw some of the fog clear from their eyes. There *was* still good in this world, and I could smile. I was looking into the eyes of the good, and it became brighter as they saw me smile for them.

It sounds so small now...but I had to take a leap that day. I had to jump into that moment, which I had almost allowed myself to miss. I didn't know how to do it without Emmett, but I had to learn to try. My babies had already lost enough. They needed me to be there for them, even if I couldn't bring them the same sparkle that birthdays had once held. I couldn't bring back their father to smile for them, so I leaped for them. I leaped into a day filled with wonder and goodness, even when all I wanted to do was to feel my own pain.

Whatever you are going through in your own family...it is unique and challenging in its own way. Sometimes our struggles are about huge issues, when we are forced to question who we are or wonder when our days will end...and sometimes, they are about simple moments...a birthday cake and a song. Some days, we are attempting to live our dreams without the sparkle we once had. But, we must remember that we are not the only ones struggling or hurting. There may be someone next door who is going through a nightmare even worse than ours. Many parts of our lives are going to be really hard, and we all have our own journeys to take, but we are not alone in our struggles. Every single person who walks this earth is going to experience life's pains and the heartache of mortality. We must realize that we are not the only ones wading through pain. For every smile that is smiled, there is also a pain somewhere inside.

We don't get to choose our trials. We do not know what tragedies lie ahead in our paths. We all have our very own "crap." Some may never be asked to share with the world what they are going through, and others might wish they could...but that doesn't take away the fact that your pain is real...and it is hard.

We don't know what others are really coping with in their lives. They might post on the web, or in public, show a side of themselves they want the world to see. Believe me, I know. I have been there! But, that doesn't mean there isn't pain and fear hiding behind their closed doors.

We see the smiles in their photos of their trip to the Bahamas...but we don't see their credit card bills that got them there, which they argue over in the late hours of the night. We see the perfect hairdos and spectacular outfits in all the photographs of their children...but we don't see the screams and tears it might have taken to get those pictures. You might stare at the online photos of the first smile of your friend's baby... and think 'what is wrong with my baby? Why doesn't she smile like that?' but you didn't see that two seconds after the smile was captured, that baby had a blow-out and got poop all over everyone in the room! You see a friend in a dream relationship...posting pictures every hour of her bliss. However, when the cameras are put away, you don't see the pain in her heart because her partner has a pornography addiction that has been tearing them apart.

We all have our struggles. It is easy to follow others on Facebook, or even in real life, and wish we had what they have. The truth is...they might be feeling the same thing, but about you! As I watched a family on television living out their every-day lives on camera, I began to wish I could have what they had. Their struggles seemed simple compared to mine. What I failed to realize was that...I was trying to live someone else's dream. I'm certain that no one watches my life and wishes it for themselves—especially the part where my husband was murdered or was cheating on me, or any of the other bumps in MY road—but there *are* people out there watching me with my five beautiful children, wishing they could just have one baby! There are people watching me who simply wish to have a child to love, and the chance to watch that child blow out candles on a birthday cake.

As I have looked back, I wish I would have enjoyed the things I *did* have much more. Before Emmett died, there were moments when I focused on his messes, or his obnoxious habits, like popping my fingers whenever he held my hand. Now, all I had left were memories and a sweatshirt. Oh, how I longed to have his crap back. If I could have all those little irritants back, I would never again be frustrated when he popped my fingers or left his wet towel on my side of the bed. I would laugh when he peed all over the toilet seat in the middle of the night. I would wash his favorite workout shirt every night so he could wear it again the next day, even though he had twenty-five more shirts in his drawer. I would cook him steak every night without complaining that I wanted something different.

What battles are we fighting with our loved ones now that, one day, after they are gone and we look back, we will miss? We will see that those battles were so small and trivial. What mountains seem hard to climb… only because we are building them ourselves? What 'crap' do we constantly complain about that really doesn't matter? Save your fights for the things that do matter, and for the people who aren't on your team. Fight less often with those who need you to see their worth, and love those more who can't find worth in themselves.

We need to stop living our lives just to take pictures to show the world… and start enjoying the moments that are real. Take pictures to remember those moments instead of staging pictures that fake them. The next time you wish you had someone else's life… remember that that person has his or her own darkness to fight. Those you might envy have their own stories, which might be more difficult to bear than your own story you are trying so hard to forget. Maybe you will never see their crap… but it doesn't mean it doesn't stink.

Even though being a parent comes with so many joys, it also holds just as many struggles and heartaches. As parents, sometimes we have to take a leap of faith and trust our children to write their own stories. As spouses, we have to jump into marriage with both feet, and trust and love. As children, we have to look to our parents for their wisdom and counsel because of their love for us and their years of experience. Taking a leap is hard. I like the power of control and knowing that I am in charge of what happens to me. But, the truth is… I am not.

If nothing else, this is the lesson I have learned. I cannot control what storms rage around me. My power lies in who I choose to become regardless of the storms. All I can do is MY best for me... and try to be there for others who are doing the best with what they have. I can give counsel and I can offer prayers... but ultimately, I have to take a leap of faith and let it go.

Doing that makes us feel vulnerable, and it is scary... but relationships are so rewarding in so many ways when you can let go of the things that are not in your control. Healthy relationships require a series of leaps of faith: faith that your partner is honest, faith that he or she will be true to you. Heavenly Father doesn't ask us to take those leaps with the promise that we will never fall. Some days will suck. Sometimes the leaps of faith will end up with us crashing, but we can't let our fears of getting tangled up stop us from living with faith. Sometimes our leaps will leave us writhing in pain... but that doesn't mean they weren't worth taking. We must do our best to give it our all. Take the Leap. Find the smile.

Parenthood is going to be hard. Just as in the TV show I had come to love, we are going to have highs and lows. The struggles are going to weigh us down at times. If you are blessed with the opportunity to live that blessing... take the leap. Give it your all. Every moment of every day, be the parent your kids deserve. Even if you are alone, without a spouse, while watching your children blow out candles on a birthday cake... take a leap and smile for all the love in their eyes as they look to you for reassurance that it *is* a wonderful world. You may be watching them alone in your pain... but you are not alone. Life's pains are all around you. Others may look like they are smiling on the outside, but inside they may be hurting just like you. Life can be exhausting, it can seem unfair... but allow yourself to live the little joys that are still all around you. Your loved ones are waiting for you to take a leap and smile for them.

Spend less time dreaming about things you no longer have, and more on the dreams you can make right now. Find joy in living the life, and being the *you* that you are today. Don't wait around to find yourself... or wait for the year that will bring you the "life you deserve." Let life deserve all of you right now. Forget about the yesterdays when it was so easy to laugh; forget about the tomorrows that might bring you brighter days; smile for the todays and the moments you stand. Smile for the family you do have...even if it is just you. You may feel lonely, you may be all you have left...so look in the mirror and smile because *you* are worth smiling for...even when there is no one there to smile back. Find the wonder in the world. You might be living the 'glory days' right now, but missing them because you are too busy waiting for them to come in the future. Don't wait to celebrate...because tomorrow might be too late. Take the opportunity to show all the eyes watching you that even when it hurts, you can still smile for them. Don't let a moment pass when you don't soak it all in. The world can be wonderful, even when it is hard. The trees might not look green from where you are standing...so find a way to take yourself to higher ground to get a different view. Take a leap and find joy as you soar...one smile at a time.

CHAPTER TWENTY-NINE

Why?

AFTER HIS FATHER'S DEATH, IT TOOK TEAGE several months before he would even go into his bedroom. I'm still not sure quite why. One day, I went shopping with my sister Ali to buy Easter presents for the kids, and I decided that rather than giving them the usual baskets this year, I would buy them new scripture cases. We picked out a case and a set of scriptures for each of my children. I even found a cool tie pin for Teage that said 'Future Missionary.' For the twins, I got them each their own mini *Children's Songbook*. They seemed like the perfect gifts this year to help the kids remember the true meaning of Easter.

As I was walking up to pay, a picture of our temple caught my eye. I stared at it for a minute. I could see the exact spot where the kids and I had sat and touched the temple wall that day not so long ago. As I walked away to go to the cash register, I was drawn back to the picture again. In my mind, I could feel the spirit telling me that we needed this picture.

I asked for the clerk to grab it off the wall so I could pay for it with the scripture cases. At $150.00, it was kind of pricey for my thrift store shopper's mentality, but I just couldn't let go of the feeling that I needed to take it home with me. When the cashier scanned it, she said, "Wow, this must have just gone on sale because it is marked down to $25.00!" I asked her to double check and, sure enough, the picture was on a huge sale that day!

As we drove home, I thought about where I should hang my new purchase. Teage's little face popped into my mind. When we pulled up to the house, I marched inside, my prize in my arms. I found Teage and asked him to come with me. We sat on the stairs right outside of his bedroom. I held up the picture. I looked into his eyes and said, "When I was out Easter shopping with Ali I saw this picture of the temple. I bought it for our family. As I drove here, I realized that Heavenly Father wanted you to have it for your room. I know you haven't gone in there for a while, and that is okay… but I want you to know that this picture is going to be hanging in there when you decide it's time to go back."

He set his hand on the picture, in the exact spot where he had put his hand on the temple wall when we had gone there. "Mom…that is where we were, right there! Remember we held our hands on the outside right there, and you and Tytus were sitting right there…and Bostyn was right here with Bailey, and me and Kaleeya were sitting right by you? Remember?…You promised we would be okay."

"I remember, Buddy. That was such a special day for me, too."

A tiny tear fell down his face, his eyes stared deep into my soul, and he said "Mom, I have an idea. What if you hang this picture down low, and then if I ever go in my room and I don't feel safe, I can just go over to it and touch my spot on the side wall right here." I had chills all over my body. "Buddy, I think that is exactly what we are supposed to do with this picture."

That night, he slept in his own room for the first time since Emmett's death. He knew he had a safe place to go when he felt scared. A few weeks went by and Teage seemed more and more settled every day with the idea of sleeping in his room. He got to the point where he wasn't afraid to go in there. He began to sleep… not all through the night, but there were stretches during the night when he actually closed his eyes and let his body relax. Baby step by baby step, our nights became smoother as he finally viewed his room as a safe haven.

One night, I sent him in to bed to read before it was time for me to tuck him in. When it was his turn, I jumped down the stairs and as I rounded the corner to enter his room... I froze in my tracks. It was like I was looking into the eyes of darkness. He almost looked evil. There was a feeling of heaviness in his room. Teage's eyes were fixed on the wall... but it was as if he was staring right through it. I sat down on the side of his bed. "Hey, son. You doing okay tonight? You seem different than when I sent you in here to read. Is there anything in particular you're thinking about tonight?"

His eyes remained fixed... looking through the wall, "Yeah." His face had no expression, just an angry scowl. "Why do police have guns?" I knew where this conversation was headed. I braced myself for tears... trying hard not to get too emotionally involved. I hadn't even said the word 'gun' in a long time. "Well, buddy... um... Police... see, they carry... um... guns with them so they can protect themselves and other people."

My heart was pounding; my throat burned. I hoped my answer would satisfy him.

"WELL... MOM... that is the stupidest thing I have ever heard. Why? I ASKED WHY, and you said 'to protect people.' Why? So if they have guns to protect people... then WHY didn't they protect DAD? WHY would they even bother carrying guns if they aren't going to use them to protect people who need protecting. If they carry guns to protect people... then why didn't they use their guns the night Daddy got shot? WHY weren't they there for HIM? WHY wasn't he good enough for them to protect? Why wasn't their gun stronger than Rob's? WHY are guns even real... and why do the stupid police even carry them, if they couldn't even protect Dad? Why would Heavenly Father give us police and GUNS to protect us if he wasn't going to ask them to protect my DAD? Why would he let Rob shoot my dad in the heart and in the head? I hate the police, I hate Rob, I hate guns. ... Heavenly Father lies... and WHY did you lie? You said they have guns to protect people. WHY would you lie to me? That isn't why they have guns or else my dad would not be dead!"

Sometimes we will have fear stop is in our tracks. Sometimes we will doubt in our core our very existence, and everything that used to make sense. Teage used to want to be a policeman, but now he had found that even they aren't perfect; even they will not be there on some dark nights to protect us; even policemen sometimes find themselves overpowered by the power of a bad guy. Where did that leave Teage's faith in the world? Lost. Unprotected. Scared. Lonely. Dark.

For the first time in his life, Teage questioned God. He wondered why his Heavenly Father hadn't sent the police with their guns to be stronger than Rob's. He asked WHY.

I realized that night that it is okay to question. It is okay to find answers for yourself. Sometimes for a night, or even for a few years, we cannot find any faith inside of us. My little boy's questions were hard for me to hear that night, but it was his questioning that made me understand that the power of my faith couldn't reassure his. He had to develop his *own* faith. He had to find answers to 'why' all on his own. He had to seek his own way to build the foundation of a testimony, not only of the law and the things of this world…but of God. I could be there to help him when he needed me, but ultimately his finding answers would have to come for him…in his own time.

We will all ask 'why' at some time or another. I have pondered over many questions. Why do we get married if that vulnerability can leave us broken? Why do we take leaps if most of the time we fall? Why bother loving if we don't always get love in return? Some might question…why do we have kids if the work is hard and the pay is nothing? Why should I believe in God? Why can't I feel God in my life? Did Jesus Christ really live? Why must we struggle? Why must people we love die? Why can't I live forever? Why do we feel pain? Why do we fight? Why should I care about others' needs, when my needs are never met? Why is the world so cruel? Whey do accidents happen? Why do bad things happen to good people?

There will be moments when we lose sight of the faith we once had.

There will be days when we stand paralyzed by fear, void of the peace we so long to feel. Teage had come so far, but that night, he almost seemed worse off than when we had started along our journey of healing. It was like for every step we had taken forward, we took ten steps back. It was getting old! Sometimes, it almost seemed easier to just give up, and spend less energy on moving forward that one step. Falling back ten was so much easier.

But eventually, for every step forward... we would only fall back nine steps... and then eight... then seven... and eventually we started to see that our baby steps forward started to carry us higher up that black mountain, the summit of which had once seemed impossible to reach.

Questioning is part of our journey; seeking answers is part of our task here on earth. Did Jesus really walk the earth? Does Heavenly Father really know me? Am I really a child of God? These are questions we all must ask, and for which we all must seek answers. We cannot progress using anyone else's faith. The answers to their questions will not answer our questions. Each of us has our own road to pave and our personal testimonies to build. Riding piggyback on someone else will only work for so long, and eventually we will come to a crossroads where we will be left standing alone. If our own faith is not strong enough... we will fall.

When the 'whys' of the world seem to weigh us down and the answers seem to be miles away... all we can do is have faith that answers will come. We must pray that our patience will lead us to the answers we seek. Faith is believing in something we do not see.

Teage didn't believe in the power of policemen's guns to keep him safe because he never saw them first hand. He had just heard that policemen were there to protect him. Just because they failed to protect Emmett that night, didn't mean that they weren't doing their best... it didn't mean that the law had abandoned us. Just like the policemen's guns, Heavenly Father isn't always going to stop us from feeling the pains or taking the bullets in our lives... but He will be there to carry us out... or carry us home.

Why? Because He loves us. He loves the homeless man in a gutter. He loves the CEO of a large corporation. He loves those who are surrounded by people who adore them. He loves the person who is all alone. The answers we seek will come. They may not come today or tomorrow...or even this year...but He will send them when we are ready for them. There are moments when even He does send them, we are too prideful or too bullheaded to accept them in the form in which they present themselves. We must stand humbly, willing to accept answers to our prayers, however they may come.

Focusing on the 'whys' of our journey will not get us far. We need to start asking 'how?' How can I believe? How can I fix this problem in my marriage? How can I be there for my neighbor who is suffering? How can I find freedom from my addictions? How can I help my husband know he is loved? How can I reassure my wife that she is enough? How can I find a way to get my seventeen-year-old to open up to me? How can I bear this physical pain? How can I help my autistic son with his struggles? How can I build a testimony for myself? How can I know I am one of Heavenly Father's children?

Asking why comes naturally...but really seeking the HOW is when our prayers can be answered. Sometimes, we are guided to the people or the doctor who has an answer for HOW. Sometimes, we are given the words to say to our teenager, or two-year-old, to comfort them in a moment when they fear the world. Some days, we will be guided to find the ways to have faith, when all hope seems lost.

Answers to our prayers do not always come as a silent whispering or a loud booming voice in a moment in our closets. Sometimes, the answers come through a picture of the temple—which just happens to be on sale—that brings peace to a four-year-old boy when all of the 'Why's' seem to leave him feeling alone. Sometimes, it is someone else's pain and questions that help us see HOW we can be there for them.

There were many moments when it was easy for me to ask God the 'why' questions. Why did I have to answer questions such as these on a continual basis? Why did I have to raise broken children who had no trust in this world? Why did I have to face reality? Why wasn't I enough for Emmett? Why didn't he tell me about what was going on? Why did Rob use a gun in his anger? Why did Emmett and Kandi hurt their spouses? Why did Rob know about the affair, but I didn't? Why didn't Rob send me that letter instead of waiting in his car with a loaded gun? Why didn't I have any answers until after Emmett was dead? Why did I have to move forward? Why did I have to get out of bed? Why did someone always seem to need me? Why did I have to feel like I was all alone? Why did I have to sit here and listen to my baby boy question God?

On that day, I didn't ask why. Instead I asked Heavenly Father HOW to answer my son...and HOW to bring peace again to my home. There are enough people in the world sitting around asking WHY. Let us be the answers they seek as we silently show them HOW. For every time we ask God WHY in our lives...let us also remember to ask him HOW. He might not answer us as to why...but He will send us ways to find the 'HOW.'

I know that Jesus Christ lives. I know He loves each one of us individually. I know He mourns when we mourn, and that He has suffered all of our pains for us. He will comfort those who stand in need of comfort. Without Him, we are nothing. He knows we will have questions on WHY we have to go through the pains of this world...but don't leave *Him* asking WHY *we* have forgotten HIM. We must turn to Him and ask him HOW we can make it through. He is HOW and He knows WHY...and he cares...because he loves YOU.

CHAPTER THIRTY

P.S...I Love You

I REMEMBER A DAY WHEN THERE WAS a really bad feeling in our house. The kids were having a hard time, and Tiffanie and I were struggling to figure out how to get everyone to calm down. At one point, Kaleeya kicked Tiffanie in the face. I grabbed her and took her up to her room. While I was upstairs, Teage punched Bostyn in the stomach. By the time I made it downstairs to try to put out yet another fire, I became overwhelmed by the crazy feeling swirling around in the air. I just stared at my children; I didn't even know where to begin to respond to them anymore. We were like a bunch of pathetic wild animals...we didn't seem to know what to do with our anger and the whirlwind of our emotions. I looked at Tiffanie and burst into tears, and then left the room and stumbled into my quiet spot in my closet.

I sat there silently sobbing, trying to think of how to make this dark feeling leave our home. I was rehearsing the events of the day— trying to understand why everyone seemed to be taking their emotions out on each other— when my sister, Ali, came walking in and plopped down next to me. She was crying as well. Apparently negative emotions were in the air for her too. She said, "I broke up with Will....He doesn't deserve to have a broken girlfriend who has no idea how to love him back." She threw her arms around me and we both cried like little babies.

I thought about what she had just said because it rang true to my own heart. I was broken...there was no doubt about it. I couldn't imagine being where she was and trying to love a man at that time in her life. We sat there for a while, just sobbing and feeling sorry for ourselves, and for each other. Our lives were stuck! She had been there right along side of me through it all...and the aftermath of our tragedy was not leaving us feeling much hope for our futures. Our roles in the story were not the same...but the pain in our hearts was intertwined. I could feel her pain as she laid her head on my shoulder, and I could almost feel her lift some of my pain from off my back.

Thank goodness for Tiffanie on days like this. *She* had been the one that just got kicked in the face, and yet she was out there taking care of the kids while I sat in my closet crying with my sister... another one of those sweet moments I will never forget. We felt as if our despair was so deep that we would never be able to rise above it, and our pain felt as though we were the only ones in the world who had ever hurt like this.

There were not many times when I shared my safe haven spot in my closet...but that day, I had a shoulder to cry on and I got to provide a shoulder for my sister to cry on as well. Without my family, I don't know where I would be today. They have brought me much of the beauty that I've found again in this world. They have been the rock I have relied on... when my foundation was crumbling. We had many good times shared with Emmett, but they have also made many new memories with me, which I will never forget.

Well, that day, the kids kept talking about how excited they were not to have school on Monday because it was Memorial Day. I had decided to just pretend that Memorial Day didn't matter to me this year. There was no way I was going to take that drive again to Emmett's grave. I hadn't recovered from the trauma of the first time we had been there, and I was determined to just have a little memorial service at home with the kids. It didn't make any sense to drive all that way...and it wasn't like he would even know of all the effort it would take. Our house felt broken. There was so much contention stirring around in it that its atmosphere felt thick and dark. The last thing we needed was to drag all of our broken selves far away to put flowers on Emmett's grave.

Tiff and I sat silently folding laundry, while the kids were spread throughout the house. All of the sudden, an impression came to my mind. I looked at Tiffanie and said, "We have to go. I need you to put all these outfits in a suitcase and find swimming suits for all the kids. I'm calling our friends, Heather and Frank, to find us a hotel. We have to go put something on Emmett's grave this weekend. The kids need to be there again…and I need to see it. That's the answer to the darkness in the house today. We need to leave as soon as our bags are packed."

Within one hour, our bags were loaded into the car and we were on our way to Logan. It was interesting to be making the trek we had made just a few short months before. I still don't have much of a recollection of that day. I had been in such a daze, and I still have no idea of how my car and all the babies inside it ever made it…knowing we were driving there to put Emmett's body into the ground.

This time was different. We had come out of our state of shock, but the thought of visiting the gravesite still left a bad taste in my mouth. The heaviness I thought would leave me as we drove away from home, seemed to linger. The reality of going to see Emmett's grave made my heart hurt. I tried to deny the fact that he was dead…and the thought that Memorial Day would always be a day when I had to think of him being gone, was a difficult one. I *wasn't* okay with the idea that we would have to stand there alone, putting flowers on his grave. It just didn't seem right…but for some reason, I longed to be there. Somewhere inside of me, I thought maybe he would be there waiting for us…or I would at least feel his presence.

We talked about life the whole way there; what life was like before, what it had become, and what I really wanted it to be again someday. I talked a lot about the memories I had of Logan and what a great time it had been for us there. I thought of all our barbecues with our friends. I reminisced about the summers spent at our apartment complex with everyone laughing and watching our kids have the time of their lives on a cheap playground set. Everything had been so simple, so wholesome, and so good. Every memory seemed bright and uplifting, and almost perfect in my mind.

I was excited to be in that little town again, and somewhere inside of me, I began to think that maybe we should move there. Looking back now, I know that I was just trying to run away from everything at home. I truly believed that by moving back to Logan, it would somehow bring me back to life. I felt that if I lived there, I would be filled with all of the good memories of the fun years Emmett and I had shared there. As we drove, I actually started making plans to find a home and move the kids to the town where Emmett and I first fell in love and began our family.

In the movie *Cloudy with a Chance of Meatballs*, there is a part where the main character, Flint, sprays his invention called 'Spray on Shoes' onto his feet and then realizes he's never going to be able to take it off again. He describes his frustration, "I wanted to run away that day...but you can't run away from your own feet!"

I would have to say there have been many moments in the last few years, when I have felt that same feeling of being trapped like Flint describes. Driving to Logan that day was one of those moments. I felt that if I moved to another city, back to a town that had brought me a lot of joy...maybe my circumstances would change; maybe all my pain would disappear.

What I know now—but didn't realize then—is that you cannot run away from your own feet! Changing your environment might make a difference for a time, but, if you don't fix what's wrong inside, eventually it will all feel the same.

When we got to the hotel that night, I realized that the next day was Sunday. We wouldn't have time to buy any flowers, go to church and then get up to Bear Lake to the grave in the timeframe we had planned. So, after the kids were all in bed, I decided to run to Walmart to pick up some flowers. Easy, right?

However, as I stood near the Walmart entrance staring at all the flower arrangements—as if they were covered in spider webs—I couldn't even bring myself to touch them. I knew if I actually picked one out, it would mean that all of this was real...and that I would actually have to drive my children to their father's grave and decorate it. If I picked out a flower wreath that said 'DADDY' on it...it really meant their dad was gone. I wasn't ready to face that reality...so I just stood there and didn't move.

I have no idea how long I had remained frozen there, with subtle tears flowing down my cheeks, when a young man walked over to me and grabbed my arm. "Hey," he said, "I couldn't help noticing how beautiful you are and I was wondering what you're doing just standing here?"

I glanced my eyes his way without moving my body...thinking, 'this poor shmuck has no idea what he just got himself into.' I wiped my face and said, "Well actually, I am trying to talk myself into picking out a flower wreath so my kids can go decorate their dad's grave tomorrow for Memorial Day." He half smiled, and said...."Ha ha, that's funny...you got me.....Wait, are you serious?...I am so sorry...how did he die?" Another deep breath. Poor kid, he was asking for it! "Well, actually, he was murdered...so, we done yet?"

I guess this guy had no filter...or maybe he actually liked being in this awkward situation with me, because he persisted. "Like, why, how...what happened? Did you know the other person?...Do they know why? Do you mind talking about it...I just...I don't know what to say..."

Apparently, in his mind, not knowing what to say meant to keep right on talking. Since I could tell I wasn't going to get rid of him easily, I just spilled out the entire sordid story. For a few minutes, I just let it all out! It felt good to get it out of my head, but weird to be telling it to a complete stranger.

He stared at me as if I were a ghost. "Wait, are you really serious? Are you making this up or...is there something wrong with you?... This isn't a funny joke."

I didn't know whether to laugh and tell him he'd just been punked, or to continue talking. "I am sorry to say I am serious…and it sucks…and I am scared…and I don't want to do any of it. Now, will you PLEASE leave so I can finish what I'm doing here?"

He started to walk away. Finally I could go back to feeling sorry for myself and wondering how to physically pick up a bouquet…or any other arrangement…off the shelf.

Again, I just stood there staring, when all of the sudden, he was back. "Hey…I believe you and I am so, so sorry…but I can't walk away from you without knowing if I could see you again.…Can I have your phone number?"

I think it took me about two minutes to comprehend what he had just asked, and to really know what to do. I blankly glared his way. "After all that…really? Why the heck would you want my number? I just told you about my crazy life…and that I have five kids and that I'm widow of someone who was murdered! He was shot because he was cheating on me.…I have a murder trial to go to in the next year or so…so why on earth would you want to ever talk to me again? What the HELL would you do with my phone number?"

He waited a minute and smiled and said very softly, "Well, you seem like an amazing person, an awesome mom, and like I said before I heard your story, I think you are beautiful."

So without a second thought, I gave him my number! After he left, I grabbed a flower wreath and went through the checkout without any more hesitation…not another minute of wallowing in my pain, or wondering how I'd get through tomorrow's events.

I don't know why I gave him my number, but it actually felt good to think that someone could see any beauty in me after hearing the truth about my past. I walked out of the store, a little wigged out that I had just told my story and given my phone number to a complete stranger…while picking out flowers for my dead husband's grave! I felt almost ashamed that I had allowed myself to say those numbers out loud...and for a moment, I had stopped thinking about Emmett.

I had parked in the middle of nowhere, so the walk back to my car was like being on a rollercoaster of excited panic and pathetic panic...alternating mode. One second, I felt like a giddy little high school girl who had just been asked out to prom...and the next second, I felt like I had just walked into my house at three a.m. and gotten caught by my Mom when I was way past curfew. I was overwhelmed with the excitement and the fear that I had done something wrong.

I finally reached the car and opened up the back to lay down the flower wreath. I hadn't paid much attention to which wreath I had actually grabbed. It was beautiful, but it was also ugly. I almost felt as if it were looking down on me for what I had just done. I slammed the trunk shut, so as not to see it any longer, then opened the door on the driver's side and plunked down into the seat. My head fell onto the steering wheel, and the tears fell onto my lap.

I felt ashamed that instead of focusing on choosing the perfect flowers for Emmett's grave, I had been distracted by this man asking questions about my tragedy and asking for my phone number. I couldn't move—I was just as frozen as I had been while first looking at the flowers. Despair set into my mind. Then as plain as day, I heard Emmett's voice—as real as if he were sitting in the passenger seat—saying: "I just wanted you to know that you're beautiful."

I lifted my head and turned toward his voice. No, it was just me in the car. I could feel him, but I couldn't see anyone sitting next to me. I sat there in the silence, trying to soak in the moment. I knew it wouldn't last long...but it was perfect. I could feel him pleading with me, "You can do this; you have to do this for them. You are an incredible mother and you are going to make an amazing wife for someone else one day." Instantly, I felt free from the torment I had allowed to creep into my mind.

In that moment, I knew Emmett wanted me to give that boy my

number. He was not ashamed that I had felt reassurance from the admiration of another man. In fact, *he* had sent him there to help me see that I *was* lovable. Emmett knew I wasn't going to snap out of my pain as I stood there—all alone—picking out flowers. No, I needed help! The flowers didn't mean anything to Emmett, they were not important. What he cared about in that moment, was ME. ... He wanted me to let go of the pain and move forward in that moment when I had been frozen in time.

I needed that day more than I will ever know. It was a humbling conversation that made me realize that I still had value; and even though Emmett had not used his last days to see my value ... I was still me. I was still desirable, and someday I was going to be capable of loving again. I may have felt broken on every level of the word ... but I was beautiful and I was lovable just the way I was ... crazy past and all. I could be adored, and desired, and I could make someone happy again. I deserved to know that I was good enough. The role I played in my past life was one I could be proud of. It was a role I played with patience, love and strength. It was a role I played with power. It was a role I played with humility. I was not perfect, but I had given it my all. I was all I had ... and it was enough. I was so grateful to know that Emmett could see that in me now ... and he was able to remind me that I needed to find it in myself again.

That was a tender mercy for me. It was the day I realized that I not only could love again ... but that I was lovable. I could be enough. And even though I was feeling like a broken shell of a person, I was still desirable and capable of someday learning how to be me again.

Every single person who has ever lived needs to know that he or she has value. Even those of us who spend months, or years, pretending that our feelings of inadequacy don't affect us need to feel that we have value ... because those feelings of inadequacy do impact us. None of us want to question our value and worth; we all want to feel special and important. We all want to feel loved. Sometimes, others are sent to remind us of how great we are ... but sometimes, there are moments when we have to stand alone and seek it within ourselves.

Don't ever let a moment pass when you see someone's beauty and you don't take the chance to tell them. If you feel someone's worth...let them know how it has impacted you. They may be frozen...trying to remember what it is inside of them that makes life worth living. Even if you never hear it about yourself, take time to show those whom you love that you believe in them. You might just save a soul; you might just be the gift of love sent from God to remind them of His love for them.

In those moments when you feel like you are trapped in your own shoes...remember that no matter how hard you try to run, you will still be you. Embrace the fact that you don't have to change everything about yourself to live the life you have always wanted. You will never abandon your own skin...so learn to see its worth. We all have goodness inside of us and all around us; Heavenly Father wants us to not only see it, but feel it. He wants us to remember to love ourselves.

There are reminders of His love and mercy all around you: the tiny voices that call out your name, the arms that reach for you, the questions asked that only you can answer, the tears shed that only you can wipe, the smiles that are smiled, the heads lying on your shoulder, the dog waiting at the door for you, the neighbor who waves every time you pass by, the old man at the restaurant who always comes to ask how your day is going and refills your drink, a breathtaking sunset, a little humming bird at your window, a gentle kiss, or a hand to hold. Even the tiniest flower is sent to beautify your environment.

Beautiful things surround you...but you might be missing them because all you see is the darkness trying to destroy beauty. In all the beauties of the earth are tiny little messages of love hidden inside. God created the earth's beauty just for you. He sent you to the family you are in... because mortality will be hard and you will need each other...but also because He wants you to experience the joy that only the members of your family have to offer. He has blessed you with the body you have, because only it could house your perfect spirit...no other body ever created could do that job for you. He has sent you to earth to live in every moment, and to magnify your days. He wants you to see your worth and the role you were sent to play amidst the beauty that surrounds you every minute of every day.

Look for the wonders of the earth; seek for the goodness of the land. Climb to the top of a mountain just to hear the silence; sail out in the waters just to see their splendor. Fly through the air and enjoy the view; watch for the majestic scenery when you drive through a mountain pass. There is grand magnificence waiting for you.

But...don't express gratitude just for the majestic beauty He has created for you...because most often, the more subtle beauties in front of you right now are often overlooked. Don't miss your baby's first smile because you are out seeking to climb Mount Everest. Don't sail away your days seeking for the grand magnificence of the earth...while the beautiful relationships you possess wait at home for you to see THEM. Let the little things be enough...and express gratitude for them every minute of every hour, for they are the beauty with which God has blessed you. Hold dear the wonders that surround you right now. If you have come to a place where others' love for you seems to have disappeared...show them a little more love, while you patiently wait for theirs to shine through once again. Just because you are in a place where you cannot see or feel love doesn't mean it is not there waiting for you. Pray for the gift to feel...beg for the gift to see.

Heavenly Father knows your heart; He sees your pain. It is through Him that we can find peace, even in our loneliest times when we stare out at beautiful flowers but are surrounded by darkness. When the darkness surrounds you...and screams to you over and over that you are not enough...don't give up on yourself. Don't let the darkness win. Watch for the tender mercies that God is trying to send just for you. Sometimes Christ doesn't have anything more for us than a shoulder in our closet to cry on, or a boy at Walmart to distract us from our pain and remind us that we are enough. Maybe in some moments, it won't be another person sent to express His love. Maybe it will come through a feeling deep inside your soul, a tender calmness to let you know that He believes in you. He loves you, and you are enough for HIM.

There are reminders everywhere … little messages that reassure you … that Christ is whispering just for you: "P.S. … I love you!"

CHAPTER THIRTY-ONE

The Road Less Traveled

THE NEXT MORNING, I WOKE UP WITH a new excitement to go to the cemetery. I guess I assumed that my special moment in the car when I had felt Emmett's presence would be continued at his grave. I was hopeful that as soon as I got there, we would share yet another special moment.

We headed out early. It was sprinkling a little bit, and I hoped that as we drove, the weather would improve. It didn't. In fact, the closer we got to the cemetery, the more the rain came down. The road up the hill to the headstones was covered in thick mud. The snow had melted, and the water that remained had turned everything to slop.

As we pulled up, I could see some of Emmett's family members already standing around his grave. I had planned on seeing them at his aunt's house later on, but inside, I felt disappointed that I wouldn't have the opportunity to be there alone with him.

It was raining so hard that the kids didn't even really want to get out of the car. What I had thought would be the perfect moment...turned out to be a dirty, cold, wet mess. I didn't get to stand over his grave and yell about all the pain in my heart; I didn't get to scream at him about how lonely I felt. I didn't get to tell him how badly it hurt that I missed him. I was longing to share all the thoughts that had been eating at me, and I wanted to ask a whole lot of 'whys.' All of those perfect words I had laid out in mind to say that day...were left stirring inside of me.

The kids came out and put the flower wreath down on the ground. Emmett's headstone wasn't up yet, and the grass hadn't had time to grow. It didn't look like a grave. It looked like a pile of mud. I had had this picture in my mind that we would sit on the grass and cry together. I thought for sure my children and I would spend all morning sharing good memories of their father. Instead we ran through the rain to throw flowers on the mud. My expectations were destroyed.

In my disappointment, we drove over to Emmett's aunt's house. It was strange being there without him. These people—whom I continued to love so much—were still sad, just like us. It was hard for me to see the pain that remained in their eyes, but in some ways, it was also a relief knowing that, like me, they were still struggling to find peace. I wasn't alone on that quest. They still had so many unanswered questions about why Rob had pulled that trigger, and why Emmett had not been at home with me that night. We didn't say a word about any of it, but I could feel it radiating from each of them.

It felt nice to be with some of Emmett's favorite people. We had built many wonderful memories with each of them. He loved them more than most people love their own siblings. They were not just aunts and uncles and cousins to him... they were all at the top of his world... they were all his family. As we left them that day, I could feel each one of them hug us with all of the love they had for Emmett. My eyes burned as I thought about all the hugs he would not get to give them and all of the memories these people would no longer be able to make with him.

We got back to Logan just in time to go to church with some family friends of Tiffanie's. I felt empty inside... still longing for the moment I had not been able to have at Emmett's grave. I felt like everyone in the church could see my pain. I was overwhelmed with anxiety... like everyone was watching me and wondering why I couldn't pull myself together, and why my kids were being disruptive and loud. Instead of finding the calmness of just being in the church building, or seeking the spirit conveyed through the talks and music, I just sat there bitter and angry. I didn't fold my arms in reverence—I crossed them in disgust.

I was so distraught about our visit to the grave, I almost considered having a do-over the next day so I could go back and try again to have the special moment for which I was still waiting. Instead, the kids played with old friends and swam in the hotel pool. I spent a lot of that weekend looking at real estate. I actually went through a handful of houses…hoping to find an answer about whether or not I should move back to Logan.

Nothing felt right. I got a few texts and phone calls from Walmart boy…but that didn't feel right either. I was so confused. My heart longed for more Walmart moments where I could tangibly feel the faith Emmett had in me, and I wanted him to continue to guide me. Why did I feel like I was back on my own again? Why couldn't he just always be in the seat next to me…helping me remember my worth and assisting me in moving forward? I didn't feel settled about anything, and I was frustrated that no answers came to help me get to where I wanted to be. It didn't feel right to move back to Logan, but all weekend, I kept trying to force it to be right.

Driving back home, I grew a little bit bitter, angry that I hadn't gotten the moment I had planned for at Emmett's grave, and disappointed that moving back to Logan had not felt like the right choice after all. If we weren't supposed to be there…then what were we supposed to be doing? I was pissed that the answer—which had felt so simple and laid out before me on our drive to Logan—now just seemed like a dream I was trying to push on my own.

On our way back home, we stopped to see Tiffanie's family. While we were sitting in their living room I said, "Hey Uncle Dave, I feel like I need a more reliable car. Don't you have a friend who owns a car dealership?" I had my heart set on getting a Sequoia. For months, that is what Emmett and I had planned on buying. Uncle Dave's friend happened to have one on his lot, so we drove over to take a look.

We pulled up to the car lot, but my eyes were immediately drawn to a giant Yukon parked right in front of us. The minute I saw it, I got chills all over my body. I had never had a spiritual experience buying a car before, and in an almost amused manner, I turned to Dave and said, "That's the car I'm supposed to buy right there, but of course I'm not going to get what I want today."

He laughed and said, "I'm not sure that car's for sale...it isn't parked by the other cars in the lot, but we can ask."

His friend walked over to us and said, "So, you want to know more about Sequoias?"

I looked at him and said, "I think that big Yukon over there is the car I'm supposed to buy. I had my heart set on your other car, but I want to look at that one first. Is it for sale?" I was pleased to learn that it was. The car had just been returned from a test drive and hadn't been put back in its proper spot.

We took it for test drive. It felt so right. That feeling I had been seeking all day...was finally here, and it was about a car? I didn't want answers about a car...I was seeking long term revelation about more important things. Buying a car seemed so insignificant and unimportant, but since I am so *not* a car person, I knew this had to be a prompting to buy this exact vehicle. It was bigger, newer, and more reliable than the Sequoia. That made me happy, knowing I would be traveling alone with the kids. I was also excited to have extra room in the car to accommodate having a friend ride with us. We had gotten to the point in our little minivan where we filled every seat.

So, I could see some good that would come from buying this new car, but I was frustrated that the questions to which I was seeking answers didn't seem to be on the list of important things with which Heavenly Father would help me.

I had no idea why I was supposed to buy *that* car *that* day, but it felt good to be making a choice that I had not thought of on my own. It didn't make a lot sense at the time, but in the weeks that followed, I came to understand exactly why I was supposed to buy that car. The entire week-end, I had been searching for BIG answers for my family. I was trying hard to force things to feel right. Moving to Logan was not the answer to my prayers. I wanted to do what was best for my family, but I was having a hard time seeing why my ideas were not right for us.

When we do His will...it can be so powerful. When we follow our own will, we will cause more pain and hardship for ourselves.

I remember a time in 8th Grade when I attended a ski club for my school every Saturday. We would meet in the school parking lot and ride the bus up to the ski resort and spend the day skiing together. I loved it every time we went, and I always looked forward to the next trip.

One afternoon, as I was preparing to head up the mountain for my weekly ski trip, my mom came into my room. She said, "Ashlee...I have a really bad feeling about your going skiing today. I don't want you to go." Well...this idea seemed preposterous to my young fourteen-year-old self. I had my mind made up, and I was not going to stay home.

However, my mom felt so strongly about it, that she wouldn't even drive me to the school. I found a ride with a friend and got on the bus to head up the hill. It was like any other normal bus trip: kids were laughing, boys were flirting, the snacks were yummy, and everyone was having a great time.

We were almost to the top of the mountain when something went wrong with the bus, and we began sliding downhill. Luckily, instead of skidding off the road, we got stuck in a snow bank. We spent that entire evening in a cold, broken-down bus, waiting for hours for the back-up bus to come and bail us out.

I didn't get back home until long past midnight...to a mother I can only assume had been praying her heart out the whole night. She threw her arms around me and said, "I am so thankful you are okay." With grate-ful hearts, we went to bed. She never said, "I told you so." She didn't rub it in my face. She just showed me how much she loved me and that she was grateful that everything was okay.

My mother taught me a great lesson that day. She had felt the inspiration that I should stay home...she had a plan for me that she knew would have been easier for me. She felt strongly about what I needed to do, yet she knew that I had to learn for myself. How much easier it would have been if I had just listened to her counsel. Why did I, as her daughter, feel the need to ignore her inspiration, and go through the pain and fear that were the consequences of my choice?

I'm certain she is not the only parent who has wondered about my choices at times. Heavenly Father knows exactly what is best for us... He has a plan based on the potential he sees in us, and He knows exactly what decisions would be best for us. But, He cannot force us to do anything we don't want to do. He will send us warnings and counsel over and over again...but eventually, we will have to choose for ourselves. He will not force us to obey His will...but He willingly sends us His counsel and advice.

When you feel you don't know which choice to make...let the Spirit guide you. He cares about all the decisions you are making, no matter how trivial you think they must seem to Him.

God wants us, as parents, to teach our children correct principles... but then at some point, we have to let go and let them govern themselves. They will learn more from their mistakes than they would from us forcing them to do what we want them to do. It would have been easy for my Mom to force me into respecting the promptings she felt about my ski trip. I would have been safe, and her worries would have been soothed for the moment. However, I wouldn't have learned the lesson about refusing to listen to the Spirit, and finding out for myself how alone I felt without that influence in my life. I needed to learn the hard way that the counsel given was for my good. I had to learn by doing—even if it was doing the wrong thing—and not just hearing what I was supposed to do.

That Memorial Day weekend, I wanted nothing more than to move to Logan...thinking it would be the answer to my pain. I truly believed the feelings I was cultivating inside myself about that plan would be confirmed by inspiration about how to make it happen. It all seemed so rational and simple in my own mind...and apparently I would have had a date (with Walmart boy) if I had moved back. Furthermore, I tried to force my own will while visiting Emmett's grave that day. I longed to hear his voice again, and I wanted my desires to also be the will of God. I was angry when my designed plan did not match His plan, because the ease and perfection of my own plan seemed to me to be just exactly the choices I should make. But, in the long run, I was able to understand that it was not what Heavenly Father wanted for me.

He didn't want me to force anything...because He was mapping out my course. At times, it felt as if I were standing on a winding road without direction or purpose, but each day, I have been blessed to see the whys of His plan for me.

Even creating and writing my blog was not my own idea. I spent hours in the temple and in my closet refuge begging Heavenly Father for a different way to find the healing that was promised me. I wrestled with the Spirit and with God's promptings, which for years, pushed me to share the darkest hours of my life and the personal lessons I have learned from them. On many occasions, I have questioned His will...and just like my patient mother, He has waited for me to see that His will is greater than my own.

Heavenly Father has a plan for each one of his children. He sees our unlimited potential...no matter where we have been or where we are choosing to go. The limitations we find in our lives are not from submitting to His will...but come from following our own or someone else's will.

There have been many moments along my path when others have set my course by the decisions or choices they have made. I don't know how this works for our Heavenly Father, but I am certain His heart hurts as

He sees us suffering the consequences of others' poor choices, through no fault of our own.

These moments serve as crossroads, when we have the opportunity to use our own agency to take a stand. At times like these, some choose to retaliate…thinking that God has abandoned them, or that He has forgotten their promised plan. Others decide to let Him steer their course. Life is not about the events in our path…it is about what we choose to tell ourselves and what we choose to do in those moments.

Even if the course you are on seems to be shattered into a million pieces…God can take those fragments and build you a new road. There will be moments when it seems like your road has come to a dead end… but you just have to keep going and most likely you will find a fork in the road. This is the crucial moment when His will stands waiting for you, because this fork is more than just a curve in your path…it is the moment when you STAND…unsure of which way to choose. One road in the fork leads you to Eternal life…and to Christ. The other leads you to endless misery and the darkness of the world.

It is in those low times of our lives that we have the opportunity to decide if we are going to put our faith in Him…or if we will forget Him and seek a road that comes with what seems, at the moment, to be more ease. The course we map out alone can, at times, feel simple and exactly where WE want to be. When we follow our own will, we don't have to worry about anyone but ourselves. We can choose what feels good in the moment. We can justify that it is our life…and we need to live it up. However, I can promise you this…eventually that selfish road will lead to self-loathing, solitude, loneliness, and depression. It may take years for the pain to come, but it will come.

Eternal happiness can never be built by man alone.

It is easy to be bitter…trust me, bitterness has come naturally for me. It is easy to be angry…it is a secondhand emotion that covers up much of the world's pain. It is easy to wallow in self-pity when life gets hard. It is easy to just keep falling, but that is not the path that leads us home to Him. It is not the road that brings healing for our pain and faith for our doubts.

The good news is that even if you have traveled down all the wrong roads, even if all the forks have lead you to more pain...your journey is NOT over. I have felt blessed because in all those times when I let the pain eat me alive...or the bitterness cause me to hate...I found the way to a brighter hour, and I fought for peace from the darkness that tried to pull me back into its murky paths. It has not been easy or natural, but it has been possible...and it has been worth it. I guarantee that if you fight the darkness every minute of every day, you can win when He is on your side. Don't spend your days trying to stand alone.

Where there is a Will...there is a WAY, and if you have to do it on your own, then it is not the right way. That way is not the promised answer if you do it on your own...if you put your will above His. Pray for the answers to be able to follow the Will Christ has mapped out for you. Don't let the ways of the world map out the roads you drive. Seek for the course that only He can navigate.

We do not have to drive the course alone....He is the mapmaker for our lives. He will navigate us home.

CHAPTER THIRTY-TWO

I Dream

ONE NIGHT AS I SLEPT, I HAD a series of dreams.

The first one was with me and Emmett and our children. It was a sunny Saturday morning, and Emmett was cleaning his new truck. The kids were playing in the street while we were outside washing the vehicle. Rob pulled up in his truck and without saying a word, he pulled out his gun and shot two bullets at Emmett. The babies and I sat there watching the entire thing...with no way to get away from it. We ran towards Rob, but he jumped back into his truck and drove away. Emmett just lay on the ground and didn't move. I fell down beside him. He had a bullet in his forehead and one in his chest. His lungs were not moving. He was covered from head to toe in blood. He was dead. I sat with my face on his chest and screamed and cried...while my babies watched. I did not wake up.

In the next dream, we were at a park and Rob walked up to us. Without saying a word, he shot Emmett in the heart and in the head. Still asleep.

In the next one, Emmett and I and had stopped at Walgreens to grab some drinks on the way to the movie theater. As we walked out to our car, there Rob was...waiting for us. Without saying a word, he shot Emmett in the heart and in the head. I still didn't wake up.

The next dream started out with us at a family reunion. All of Emmett's family was gathered at the cabin on Bear Lake. We were laughing and talking, and the kids were running around everywhere. It was a

perfect day, just like many others we
had spent at the lake. We were all
getting ready to head down to the
water when a truck pulled up.

Without saying a word, Rob
got out of his truck and ran toward
us. By now, I knew what was coming and I started to scream. "Rob...
No...please, please let this just be a
dream....Please stop. Just talk with
him Rob...and he will listen. I am
right here, I need you to stop. Rob, I
know you are scared. I know you are
hurting...but please put down that
gun and look at me. You have never met me before...but I know why
you are here...and I need you to stop. I hope this is just a dream. Please
Rob...I am begging you. I need him....

Please don't shoot!"

All of Emmett's family members were frozen. They had no idea of
what I knew was coming. It was like everyone was moving in slow motion: Rob running toward Emmett, my words, his family looking at me
like I was crazy, and the kids following me as I chased him. Without saying a word, Rob took out his gun and he shot...in slow motion...two
bullets. One hit Emmett in the head...and I watched it sink into his skull.
The next bullet came immediately afterwards, and I saw it pierce Emmett's skin and sink deep into his heart.

Wake up Ashlee...Please wake up. This is just a dream. It isn't real. Everything is going to be okay. You just have to WAKE up. I couldn't wake
myself up. I walked around, and everyone was still moving in slow motion. Every tear fell like it was made of syrup. Every scream was drawn out
and deep. The pain inside of my heart felt as if I were watching all of these

people grieving for the very first time. We sat there on the beach staring at Emmett's dead body, with no one knowing what to do. Our five children knelt at his side weeping tears over his dead, lifeless body.

When I finally woke up, I lay back in bed, sick to my stomach. That dream wasn't real...but the ending *was* real, and it had already happened. Emmett *had* been shot by a gun: once in the heart, and once in the head. As much as I tried to ignore it, that fact was real...and that was why he was gone.

I had a dream...but it wasn't a dream for the betterment of this world, or a dream where I could make a difference for anyone. No I had a dream that haunted me. Its power weighed heavily on my mind. Emmett was gone...and that wasn't going to change. No matter how many times my dreams tried to change the scenario...the ending was always the same.

I lay in my bed for a long time...not knowing how to get out of the horrible cycle. I thought of all my life's dreams that had been shattered by those two bullets. I thought about the hopes that had built my family and the dreams for our future, which were now just a distant memory.

I can remember exactly where I was, when as a young teen, I experienced the moment when my dream was written. I was sitting in a Young Women's class and we were talking about setting goals and reaching for our dreams. Our teachers had given us a photo of ourselves with a transparent picture of the temple covering our photo. I knew right then and there that I would not give up until all of my dreams had been fulfilled. On that day, I wrote out in my mind a laundry list, a bucket list, of all the things I would do before I died.

Getting married was at the top of it my list. I had dreamed of the life I would have as a young mother and an adoring wife. I imagined what my children would look like, and I pictured growing old one day and becoming a grandmother.

I never dreamed of having anything more than the life I actually had on the afternoon of March 11, 2011. I was living my dreams. I never wanted to change the world or become the first female president. I never hoped to run a corporation. My dreams were about dirty diapers and spit-up on my shirt. I had dreamed of being surrounded by little arms that needed me in every way. I even loved being a poor student with Emmett. I *wanted* to struggle through school together…because that meant we needed each other. I loved that we had lived in tiny apartments with a bunch of little kids. We had cooked Top Ramen and eaten it by candlelight. We had pinched pennies to buy bookshelves from thrift stores. My dream had always been to have my own garden and to teach my babies how to make things grow. I loved preparing meals and scrubbing floors. I dreamed of nothing more than a simple life…and it was right there. I had it. I had reached my dream.

On that fateful day, I spent my morning picking out laundry baskets for a new and improved laundry system I had developed for my newly-expanded family. I was so excited to have matching baskets in which I could organize and separate everyone's laundered clothes. As I walked to my car—giddy that I had found exactly what I'd been looking for—I couldn't wait to show my purchases to Emmett…and I hoped the baskets would be as exciting to him as they were to me.

However, what I didn't know as I skipped to my car that morning, was that my dream to make my laundry room beautiful and new…would be a dream I would never have the opportunity of sharing with my husband. He would never see those baskets full of clean clothes that I couldn't wait to show him. That little dream…was one I would never enjoy.

I remember a few times as a child going to a Broadway show with my father called *Les Misérables*. It has become one of my all-time favorite memories with my dad, and I have grown to love the show's music and storyline. It is about a man who went from being a prisoner to becoming a prominent and successful businessman in his society. There is one particular song from *Les Misérables* that has come to my mind a lot in the past three years, a song, which unfortunately, I have been able to relate to on many levels.

One of the female characters in the musical, Fantine, sings about the dreams she had hoped for as a young woman, after those hopes have all been destroyed. *I Dreamed a Dream* speaks to every heart that has ever felt like they have lost a vision of a life they once longed for.

At times, life *will* seem to kill our dreams. The night Emmett was shot in the heart and head will forever stand in my memories as the pinnacle moment of losing my dreams. It was my darkest hour. It was the moment when I lost hope in all my plans . . . and the moment when all the darkness of the world seemed to destroy the passion I had for any dream I have ever hoped to achieve.

We all have dreams we hope to realize. We spend our lives creating them in our minds . . . praying they will all come true. Some of these dreams will remain inside of us . . . while others will play out just as we planned.

There will be many of us who wait a long time for our biggest dreams to come true, and there will be times when we aren't able to achieve even our smallest dreams. Life doesn't always wait around and ask us what our dreams are . . . because usually, life just happens.

Some of us might have every single dream we have ever wished for when we've blown out a candle or wished upon a star . . . unfold before our very eyes. Everything we ever thought we wanted . . . actually staring us in the face. We have our dreams in our laps . . . and everything feels close to perfect. Aside from the fact that in his last few months, Emmett seemed to be struggling with what I thought was a mid-life crisis . . . I had reached that point. I was living every single dream I had ever dreamed. I was scrubbing toilets and I was buying laundry baskets . . . and it was amazing. I was living my dreams . . . but on that horrible night, all of those dreams were shattered by two shots of a gun.

Dreams can be as big as five kids and a mini-van . . . or as small as celebrating the hard work of redoing your laundry room. It doesn't matter how small our dreams seem to others, they are all significant to us. That is what makes them OUR dreams. We made the plans, we had the hopes... and we are making them happen.

Some walk this life constantly seeking a dream they may never receive; sometimes even the worthy goals we set for ourselves will not be met on this earth. The yearning for a dream that may never come is a lonely cry. At some time or another, we will all experience the moment when we realize that a dream we have been seeking will never be, or when a dream we have lived is lost forever. It is a desolate feeling that you can only understand after you have been there... standing alone.

Dreams will come every single night as we sleep... but other kinds of dreams will also be in our minds, as we hope for bright future paths to walk.

Christ's love for you is not based on your merits in mortality, and He doesn't love you any more just because you reach your goals. He may be excited that you have worked hard and have consequently received certain blessings, but His love for you is not because of your titles, degrees, recognitions, or medals. His love is unconditional. He loved you long before you even set your goal. He believed in you before you got the prize. He saw worth in you long before you gained the recognition, earned the degree, or received the title.

Heavenly Father knows there are moments when you stand alone... feeling like you haven't accomplished any of the things you set out to do when you were younger. He hurts that you cannot see your worth even when you have not achieved the merits you seek. He isn't sad that you aren't where you want to be... He hurts because you can't see that where you are is enough.

Even if every dream you have ever hoped for feels like it is impossible... or if every dream you have ever lived... feels like it has been taken away... you haven't reached the end. Tonight as you go to sleep, a new chapter of dreams might begin. Don't spend your life waiting for the dreams you long to be living; live the dreams that you wake up with each morning. Don't wait for your dreams to come true to see His hand in your life. Yes, it is good to have goals and hopes for yourself...but don't let the dreams that remain to be achieved...hold you back from living the roles you are playing right now.

Dreams are meant to add to your happiness...not to be the goal you must achieve before you can be happy. Happiness is where you are, right now, today. Maybe you are working at a job you hate with people who annoy you. Maybe you are "just" a mom and you dream of a life that you see on the big screen. Maybe you are a dad who wishes your kids could see how hard you work for them. Maybe you are a single parent doing it all alone...with no one there to cheer you on or give you praise for your sacrifices. Maybe you are a grandma who lives across the ocean from any of the tiny hugs you long to receive. Maybe you are a young high school boy who sits alone in your room...wondering why you don't have any friends, or a teenage girl who has never had a first kiss. Maybe you are a lonely man sitting in a jail cell wondering why you made the decisions you made that got you there. Whoever you are and wherever you stand... find a reason to smile. Today may be all you have left of the dreams you have already achieved.

Those dreams that night freaked the crap out of me. They shook me to the core for days, but one thing they helped me realize is that it could have been worse. What if Rob *had* brought a gun to our house and we had all been forced to watch as he shot Emmett? What if we *had* been at a family reunion and Emmett's cousins and aunts and uncles had witnessed his death? Our story was tragic...but what if it had been even more tragic? I came to understand that its plot was the simple version of what could have been even worse.

Life is going to be hard. It is going to knock you down. There will be days when you will not see the good in the moments you stand...but eventually, you can still find a reason to smile again.

I have a dream that one day, selfishness will not destroy families. I have a dream that we will be true to the promises we make. I have a dream that people will be real, honest, and kind. I have a dream that no one will ever feel abandoned, rejected, or not good enough. I have a dream that the people of this world will fight the darkness that tries to destroy us... and hold fast to the power that can make our dreams come true. Dreams never die.

There will be days when it feels like all of your dreams are lost. You may be standing in your darkest hour right now... waiting for hope that even your smallest dream can still exist. I promise you that better days await you. Don't give up on yourself... and don't give up on the light that is still all around you. Even if every dream you have ever dreamed seems to have been shattered before your eyes... you still have a reason to live. You are enough... all by yourself. Jesus Christ has felt your pain. He has heard your cries. He knows where it hurts... because he has been right where you are. Don't give up on Him. He is right there. Pray for the light to help you see His hand extended to you through the darkness. And when you find it... grab on and never let it go. He will carry you to the dreams *He* has prepared for you. They may be different from the ones you planned for yourself... but they will be perfect, because His plan is greater than any we could create for ourselves. He is the healer of our pain and the writer of our script; live the dreams he has orchestrated just for you.

CHAPTER THIRTY-THREE

Gravity

THERE CAME A TIME WHEN THE ATTORNEY General's office contacted me about participating in a Grand Jury. I didn't know exactly what that meant, or what my role would be. They explained to me that it was kind of like a practice for the real thing; almost a mock trial to see what facts they had and how a jury would sentence the accused with the evidence they had collected. It sounded like a good way to see how prepared the prosecutors were to try Rob with the evidence and facts about the case they had gathered. I knew the defense would be requiring me to take the stand at the actual trial, and that thought was frightening, but I even felt anxiety about participating in this practice trial for the prosecution.

I was afraid of the unknown. I spent the next few weeks nervous and skeptical about the questions I would be asked to answer. I imagined the moment over and over; I even asked myself questions and practiced my replies. They were always playing inside of me; it was like a weight that held onto my ankles and squeezed my heart everywhere I went. These questions were always in the back of my mind. I rehearsed in the shower, I stumbled over them as I changed diapers. Any moment when I was alone in the car, I would cry my answers out loud... usually ending in screams and anger, overwhelmed by the thought of taking the stand.

I was paralyzed by the fear that seemed to have taken over my thoughts. I went over and over all my memories of that night. I wished so badly that it had all been different, but the truth was what I had to state. I hated that the truth was so hard, and so humiliating. I knew I had to be prepared if I was going to be able to get on that stand and not break down. I knew it wasn't the real deal, and that it was just a practice for the trial… but I worked myself up about it night and day.

I was very nervous about going to the courthouse. I was afraid that I would be there at the same time as some of the other witnesses. In all of our conversations about my participation, I made it very clear that I did not want to have even the possibility of running into Kandi in the halls.… I wanted to be in the building at different times than her. They assured me over and over that that would be the case.

An attorney friend of mine made arrangements to drive me down to the courthouse on the day the Grand Jury was set to take place. I was told they would start with Kandi's testimony—since she was the only witness of Emmett's death—and they would end with my testimony, Emmett's wife. They had asked me to arrive around 2:00 p.m.

When we got to the office of the Victims' Witness Coordinator, I was so scared that I was shaking. The thought that Kandi had been in the office earlier that day made my stomach turn. Since Emmett's murder, I had not been in public once when I hadn't searched for her. I looked in every car that passed me, making sure we were not driving on the same road. I hadn't gone anywhere without the fear that we would meet, and now, here we were in the same building… on purpose. It seemed out-of-this-world and unreal that if, by chance, I took the wrong elevator or went down the wrong hallway… we could actually meet face to face.

The girl in the front office told me to sit in the waiting room chairs. The coordinator finally made her way up to tell us what was going on. She looked distraught, "Hey… I am so sorry that we had you come this early. She is still on the stand and she has been for hours. We are just scratching the surface of what they need her to share. You will have to wait here until she is done, and the other witnesses get their chance to take the stand

and be questioned. We still have you on the schedule as the final witness."

So I waited. My heart pounded and my body shook as I sat in the quiet, alone with my thoughts.

Everyone in that courtroom was being told facts that I didn't even know: facts about how my husband died, truths that only Kandi knew. I didn't know anything. I hadn't yet learned that Emmett had driven her in his car, and that they had spent the evening together before they met up with Rob at Walgreens. I hadn't learned that the two men didn't even touch each other when Rob confronted Emmett. I didn't hear Emmett's last words. He wasn't there to fight for me. I didn't hear the gun shots or see the blood dripping from his wounds. I wasn't there to hold his head as he took his last breath... but she was there.

I hated the fact that as I sat up in this quiet office waiting, she was sitting in front of a group of people telling them all the things *I* didn't even know. I hated the fact that complete strangers were in there being given the answers to all the questions that still played out in my nightmares. They were getting answers to the questions they asked... while I sat in silence.

What seemed like hours passed, and my turn finally came. I was almost excited as I walked into that room full of strangers. They didn't know me.... I was just another victim to them. They hadn't sat in my living room, on my black couch, with the detectives that night. They didn't see the looks on my babies' faces when they were told that their dad had been shot; they hadn't seen the tears running down my cheeks for weeks after Emmett's murder. It was almost as if I couldn't wait to let it all out... and show them that *this* victim still had a voice. That gun had nearly destroyed me... but I still had a pulse.

I raised my hand and promised to tell the truth, and nothing but the truth. With my heart pounding, I took my seat.

"Please state your full name." I opened my mouth to speak... but my emotions began to take over, and no words came. The bailiff asked me to repeat.

"Ashlee Corrigan... and then I spelled it: A S H L E E C O R R I G A N." My voice cracked as I pronounced each letter; it was as if my mouth were filled with saltine crackers. My throat was so dry, and the words that rolled around inside of it had no way to get out.

As soon as my name left my lips, my eyes began to burn. How could this be real? This *couldn't* possibly be my life I was going to be questioned about. It *couldn't* be my husband who died. ...This *wasn't* our story! Suddenly, I didn't want to be here. The fight or flight mechanism programed inside of me set off its alarm... and I started to panic. The attorney could tell I was losing it. He said, "You are a little emotional.... Are you doing okay?... Do you... want..."

I tried so hard to get my voice to come out again. "Yes, I just... this is... I... I... I... I will be fine." I was shaking hysterically. I took a few deep breaths, hoping to put on my smile and not let my completely distraught internal freak-out be witnessed by all.

Everything inside of me wanted to scream. I wanted to tell them everything that WE had been through... everything I had been forced to witness my kids live through. I wanted to shout about all the nights I had been tapped on the shoulder, and about all the tears that had been shed by me and by my children huddled together in my bed. I wanted to let all these strangers know that I wasn't just a victim... I was me... I was his wife... I was the mother of his babies. And we were still here... and we were still trying to figure out how to live. We had been forced into accepting our sentence. We hadn't chosen this life... and they all needed to know about it!!! Forcing myself to be silent, I sat... and waited for my opportunity to let my voice be heard.

The jury was told they could ask me any questions they wanted. I don't really remember much about their questions or any of my answers. I have no idea of how long I was there or how many questions I answered. I know that I spoke a lot about the events of that night, before he left our house. My soul ached for the Emmett I loved, as I told the story about the last words he spoke to me. My heart broke because of the unavoidable truth...that it had been *her* he was fighting for, not me.

I never did get to say all that was in my heart; their questions didn't allow my needs to be fulfilled. All they needed to know about is what transpired that night. The questions seemed to finally slow down, and I thought my time on the stand was coming to an end. My body began to settle down.

And then it came: the question I knew I would have to answer...the question to which everyone wanted to know the answer...the question I will never forget. "Before your husband died, did you know that he and Kandi were having an affair?" Everyone froze...

I looked around the room. Every set of eyes was staring at me. Those eyes seemed to be boring in deeper than my skin; they were fixed on my soul. Everyone in the room waited...

As I answered, everyone's eyes dropped. All of the sudden, nobody could look me in the eye!

I felt almost ashamed of myself. How DID I NOT know? What was wrong with me? They all seemed to be looking around the room wondering how the heck I could be married to this man...who died because of this affair...and I DIDN'T KNOW?!!!!

This group had been sitting here all day listening to the obvious facts about how my husband had been cheating on me, and how he had died. They knew everything that *I* hadn't learned before Emmett died. I stared at all their darting eyes, knowing they must have finally learned the truth about me....I WAS stupid. The facts were as plain as day, and I had missed them when they were right in front of me. I was living them...but I was too stupid to figure them out.

I could see the thoughts of the members of the Grand Jury, as if they glared out of their eyes as they focused on everything in the room...but me. "She should have known...and if she'd had any brains, she would have."

I walked out of that courtroom feeling depressed and alone. The findings of the Grand Jury that would come to settle the minds of the prosecutors, only set off more alarms of fear in me. I walked out of that courtroom even more humiliated than before. There was going to be a murder trial…and it wouldn't involve just a small group of random strangers staring at me and wondering how the crap I didn't know…it would be the whole town…and eventually, the entire country.

That night as I lay in my bed, I replayed all the questions over and over in my mind. How I wished I could change my story. I could pretend I knew about the affair; I could say that Emmett had been at home fighting for me that night before he left. I longed to tell the town that I wasn't as stupid as I looked. I had known there was something wrong, and I had been trying hard to figure it out…but I just hadn't put all the facts together in time. That night, I drowned in my tears as I considered how to change my past to make myself feel better about it…and to reassure myself that I wasn't dumb.

The next morning, I kept having this urge to go downtown again. Ha! That was the last thing I wanted to do. In the days that followed Emmett's murder, I had placed holds on all of our accounts, but I had yet to go down to the bank to make sure everything was secure. It was just another thing on my "to do" list that I had purposefully avoided in a feeble attempt to pretend that none of what I was going through was real.

By late afternoon, I knew I couldn't fight the urge any longer, and I made the decision to drive down to our bank. I was nervous the whole way there. I didn't want to talk about financial matters; I didn't want to see people who knew Emmett at the bank…and I certainly didn't want to go into a public place where more people would find reasons to remind me of how stupid I was.

I parked my car outside the bank and walked inside. I asked to speak with the man who had helped me place holds on all of our accounts. The minute we sat down in the privacy of his office, he said, "I was literally going to call you this afternoon. Earlier today, another woman was in here trying to make withdrawals from these accounts. I am so glad you came in today."

My heart dropped. My mind freaked out. I wasn't safe...in any way. Now, not even *my* bank accounts seemed to provide me any security. My fear of the unknown seemed to be multiplying and invading every dark corner I had forgotten to check.

That day, I closed every single account. Maybe that was irrational... maybe I was just being stupid like everyone seemed to think I was, but in that moment...it was my only option. I had to protect the assets I had left. For me, that meant making some big decisions in literally just a few seconds. I had felt inspired to go to the bank that day, but I hadn't realized that it was going to result in my finding even more reasons to doubt the world.

When I look back on those dark moments...it was like I was living in a haze. I thought I had made it past the hardest days...but then, something else would come along to pull me down even more than before. The force that tugged me down was stronger than just a sensation of falling. It felt like a darkness blacker than anything I had felt on earth was trying to suck me in.

The scientific definition of gravity is: the powerful force that attracts a body to the earth. During those dark days, it wasn't just the force of gravity that held me, and it wasn't just grounding me. No, it was a power that was pulling me down...down...down.

Everything I once thought was a given, seemed so uncertain. I was scared. I was stupid, and I was alone. My bank accounts were not safe... and somewhere between teaching my children how to properly grieve and function in their lives...we were going to have to live through a murder trial. I was going to have to take that stand again and tell the world all that I *didn't* know. All those things I once counted on to be constants in my life... now seemed to be not only undependable...but worse than that, they were failing me.

I wasn't even sure if the natural law of gravity was going to be a constant for me... because I could not see where on the earth I was still connected to it.

There is a force in this world even stronger than the constant force of gravity. It is a darkness that swirls around us... and even when we feel we have been pulled farther down than we knew was possible... it tries to wrench us under even further. I was surrounded by darkness on those days, and there was no place inside of me that remembered that God was still there. I did not feel Him by my side as I sat at the bank and was told that I couldn't even depend upon my bank accounts. I didn't feel Him give me a voice as my heart pounded out of my chest so forcefully that I couldn't breathe while I was speaking the truth on that witness stand. The truth was destroying me inside... but there was nowhere to hide from it. I felt completely alone and I felt scared to death.

The darkness of this world seemed to be chasing me, knowing I was weak, and I was buying every word of it. I didn't know how to keep ahead of the darkness. Fear was my motivating factor. It drove me to arise in the morning and it kept me from falling asleep at night. I could barely eat, and I had to force myself to move. Every day, I spent hours replaying the questions that were asked as I sat on the witness stand, and I knew that the questions that would be written for me at the actual trial would be even more difficult. They would pull me down with even greater force.

Every single day... being pulled down... thinking; rehearsing; practicing; hallucinating... and feeling scared, but most of all humiliated.

There are many powers that pull at us: Hate, Pride, Fear, Jealousy, Anger, Doubt, Rage, Humiliation, Despair, Pain, Rejection, Doubt, and they are all powers of darkness. Darkness is always waiting to grab us in its clutches; it always knows just how to make its lonely walk... and it has the ability to make us long to join it for that walk. It waits for us along all the roads we tread and at all the crossroads where we stand alone. It is not willing to sacrifice for us, but it *is* willing to sacrifice US for the power it wants to hold over us. Satan is not constant.... He doesn't stick around when we reach our breaking point. He walks away when he gets us to the spot where we cannot stand, and he hopes we will forget the light we once had. More than anything, he wants us to give up and forget. He willingly takes control when we feel we have lost it. The only thing that is constant when he steers our course... is our ultimate defeat. He promises nothing more than his own gain.

However, we don't have to choose to fall under his power... for he will only bring us down. We are the ones who hold true strength... and darkness can only control us if we give our power away.

God's love for us is the constant we must seek. Its power is the force that can keep us grounded. Even in the moments when we stand and feel that all the truths we once thought were consistent are falling through our grasp... He is still there. I didn't let Him comfort me in that courtroom that day. I let other forces pull me down. I let fear take control of my body in every car I rode in and in every elevator I exited. I sat at that bank feeling alone and overwhelmed by darkness.

Gravity is a force that exists no matter what we do. We can try to fight it... we can try to pretend that its power cannot control us... but ultimately, no matter how many times we try to leap off that barn's rooftop... we will fall to the ground. No matter how many times we try to fly out of that tree... we will hit the grass. Gravity was created for us for that purpose. Our questioning its existence will in no way change its power. It will always be there.

However, our Heavenly Father is just as constant as gravity. He is always there. He walks with us into all the 'banks' that threaten our peace and make us feel like our security is about to be destroyed. He helps us close the accounts when we are not safe. He wipes our tears when the humiliation of the world tries to make us feel like we are stupid, and He is holding us up when we feel we cannot take another breath... as we speak the truth.

I have no idea why I wouldn't allow myself to see His power in those moments, but I could easily feel the darkness. Looking back, I guess I needed to forget His love momentarily so that I would be driven to remember how to fight for it again. I thought I was walking all alone. The days when, in my mind, I was traveling solo...served as anchors to tug at me and remind me to seek His light again.

There are powers that pull us to and fro; there are forces that try to bind us. When we seek for the power that comes from the goodness inside of us...and from the Love of our Savior, that is when our paths seem to be surrounded by the hope we seek. Darkness will never bring us peace; it will never leave us full of happiness.

My hope in myself was lost; my hope in this world seemed to be impossible to find...but somehow, it found me. I didn't seek it on those days full of darkness...but it was still there.

Gravity will hold you anchored to the earth, but only Christ will keep you grounded as you travel along life's roads. Let the power of His mercy be the one that anchors your ship when the storms of the sea try to shake you. Let the gravity of His love hold you to the truths that only He can teach. You are smart. You are enough. You are the *you* He always wanted you to be. You have the power to choose the light.

Don't let your fear of walking alone keep you from taking the next step. You are not alone. He is there. His power is real, and He holds it just for you. Gravity may bring you down, but Christ's love can lift you higher.

CHAPTER THIRTY-FOUR

The Way We Deal

THE LAST PRESENT I GOT FROM EMMETT was a pair of running shoes. It was probably about two weeks before he died. He came in late one night from work and threw the box toward where I was sitting on the couch. I picked it up and said, "What are these for, Em?" He replied, "You said you want to feel like you are loved...so there you go."

I stared down at this expensive pair of shoes; they were shiny and new. I had wanted a pair of lavender shoes at the store a few months before, but these were bright blue. I searched the box for what I was longing to find inside...LOVE. After I removed the shoes from the box, only tissue paper remained. Nothing inside that box gave me the feeling of love that I wasn't feeling in my marriage.

In that moment, I realized that my desire to feel love through Emmett's time and emotional connection was not something I was going to be receiving. I tried so hard to see where inside that box full of 'stuff' I could feel his love for me. He didn't, after all, have to buy me these shoes or take the time to bring them home to me. Yes, I guess—somewhere intermixed in my apparent despair for the feelings I was not receiving—I found myself holding tight to the love that had deceitfully put itself inside of a box.

I have never been the type of girl that could be bought; gifts have never been my love language. Emmett, on the other hand, had experienced much of his love coming in the form of gifts. That was one of the ways he showed love, and the way he knew how to receive it. I didn't relate to this form of love through either giving or receiving gifts. I wanted to feel Emmett's love through his actions; I wanted to hear it in his words; I wanted to see it in the time he spent with me...and I had no idea how to show him love through purchases or things.

The different ways we show and are able to receive love are not bad... they are just different, but as I sat on the couch that day with the shoes on my lap, I almost burst into tears. I longed to be held in his arms and to be told how much I meant to him. These shoes, to me, were just reminders of the time we were *not* spending together. I didn't need new shoes to be happy. We had spent years together with no money...and I had loved every minute of it. We had found love in the simple pleasures and kind words of our days; we had found peace in the small embraces and tender moments of being with our family. In my mind, it was money that had ripped us apart.

The day after Emmett was shot, and the kids had been told he was gone, the house felt scary and empty. There was an eerie feeling from which I wanted to run. My friend Emily and my sister Ali were sitting with me in the living room, when all the sudden, I had to get out of the house. They said they would come with me. We drove. I yelled. I cried. I don't even remember all that I said, or all that I did...but they just silently listened. I screamed at Emmett; I yelled at Kandi; I cried for Rob and the pains that must have put that gun in his pocket. I cursed that gun; I swore at the air...I pounded the dashboard.

When my fits came to an end, we were still driving and I craved a taste of normal life. Soon, I had talked them into going into Costco with me. I walked into the store in a daze. I had made up my mind that I was going to buy the new vacuum I'd been wanting. We walked up and down the aisles. With every row I went down, I became more and more aware of the fact that I was losing it. Why one earth was I making myself walk around Costco? I was trying so hard to be normal...and yet inside I was dying.

I turned a corner and there was the mother and sister of one of

Emmett's best friends. They said hello and gave me a hug. I could tell they had not heard the news. I burst into tears. Even more out of my mind, I said, "Emmett died...he died last night...I have no idea what the heck I'm doing here...just had to get out of my house and I need a vacuum... and he died, he got shot last night at Walgreens. I can't sit in that house any more today...I don't know why I am here...I just...I just need, I needed a vacuum."

They were in shock; they had no idea. Their expressions matched my feelings inside...like, 'what the heck is she doing here?' I was wondering the same exact thing. A vacuum...really? It couldn't wait for another day? What *was* I doing here? Why did I think that stepping into the store where I've spent many normal days would all the sudden make everything right inside of me?

Grief and fear were like a plague causing me to lose control over any rational thought I had left. And Costco was just the beginning of the many searches I would take to try to find the missing pieces of my heart.

I was returning from downtown one day after a particularly long afternoon talking about elements of the murder trial, I was at a low point. I had just gotten off the freeway when an RC Willey furniture store caught my eye. I pulled into the parking lot and threw my car into park. I marched inside and searched. Somewhere inside this building there had to be something I could buy that would make me feel better about my life... something they had to offer just had to be the ticket to what I needed.

And there it was: a giant entertainment center! Emmett and I had been talking forever about how much we wanted a huge, black entertainment center for our living room. I walked up to the clerk, and within minutes I was writing a check for three thousand dollars. I was so excited for it to be delivered; I couldn't wait for it to be set up so I could admire its magnificence.

The delivery day finally arrived, and it was brought in piece by piece. The delivery men assembled it and got my TV hooked up perfectly. It did look amazing, that was for sure. It seemed to be worth every penny I had paid. It was beautiful, and I was so proud of the fact that I had bought it all by myself.

That night when my house was quiet and everyone else had gone to sleep, I sat on my black couch to admire my purchase some more. It was astoundingly breathtaking; it was just as I had always pictured it would be. I didn't move, just took it all in...waiting for some positive emotion to fill my empty heart. I longed for the feeling I thought it would bring... but it never came. The house was still empty, the room was still lonely, and my heart still hurt.

This expensive, massive collection of wood didn't come with a promise of joy... it wasn't surrounded with love. It was just a big, giant THING. It wasn't capable of receiving or giving me any of the tender moments I wanted it to share. That feeling I had inside of me, the one screaming for attention... it was still there. Nowhere inside did anything change for me that night, except for the feeling of regret that I had been looking for the love I still sought... in a giant, overpriced stack of wood.

To anyone who has ever felt afraid, alone, or filled with grief or re-morse—so to all of us who have ever lived— sometimes we just have to deal. Our emotions have to find their own way of coping. Some people deal with sadness by eating; others cope with grief by diving into work. Some buy new cars or move to bigger houses; others shut out everyone else. Some search for peace in drinking; others can't seem to make them-selves even leave their homes. Some of us smother the people around us to try to squeeze out every ounce of love they have for us; others grab onto something that isn't really theirs to take.

On some days, I dealt with my grief by searching in stores. I went to Costco the day after Emmett died... not to buy a vacuum, but to search for something I thought I might find to fill my emptiness. I ordered an en-tertainment center, not because I needed it or even really wanted it... but because I was hoping for a happiness that I didn't seem to have at home. I bought clothes for the kids and knick-knacks for my house. I spent hours rearranging furniture compulsively, and moving kids to different rooms, not because I hated the way the house looked...but because I hated the way I felt inside.

I have never been one who could be bought off or who loves gifts. All of the sudden, I craved the type of "love" Emmett had given me, which was now gone. That was one of the ways he had shown me love...and now I found myself searching for love in things. My gifts to myself never once brought me any lasting peace or love, but I didn't know where to look...and I couldn't find it anywhere else. I searched the stores for love, and each time I came home with a package that was void of it, and my loneliness was accompanied by regret.

One of my favorite movies in the entire world is called *The Ultimate Gift*. It is about a young man whose grandfather passes away and instead of just giving his grandson his fortunes, he sets up a series of events for his grandson to learn to appreciate what he already has. It is an amazing movie that teaches the lessons of being grateful, learning to serve others, and finding yourself. In the end, the ultimate gift turns out to be way more than money or things...it is a change that the grandson finds inside of himself...a change in his heart.

Our desperate desire for love, and our longing for healing will not come from the things of this world. First, we must change the way we view ourselves; we must seek for a power greater than those of this world to help us see our purpose in it.

It is easy to buy things to show our family members that we love them. After all, we work hard for them to have the things they need. We go to school to become capable of providing for them and then we go to work to make money and become successful. Shouldn't that be enough? Shouldn't the fact that the clothes they are wearing, and the food they are eating come from our paycheck be enough for them to know that someone loves them? It would seem that that could be true...but it isn't. Our families need more than a paycheck and bank account to feel our love for them.

Our children deserve to know that at the end of every day, the ultimate gift we are giving them is more than just money and things...they want ALL of us. They need our smiles; they want our time; they desire our hearts. It may be grand that they are being tucked into bed in a four thousand dollar California King...but if our hands are not the ones that pull up the silk sheets around their necks...do you really think they care about how much the bed cost? They may act like they enjoy the new set of wheels they are driving, but if we aren't there to teach them how to drive it...do you think it is the car they will remember?

They don't want your money. Maybe on the outside they ask for it, even beg for the 'things' that fill up their days...but on the inside...all they want is YOU.

Gifts are fun; toys are exciting; new cars are thrilling; a giant house is amazing; every guy loves a new TV in his bedroom; every girl craves a new pair of heels...but what they really NEED...is you.

We all need to hear that we are enough; we need you to show us that we are worth your time; we long to see you check us out from across the room. We crave to be looked into the eyes and told we are beautiful, or handsome, just the way we are. To me, that is the ultimate gift. The gift of love.

Things will not bring you the happiness for which you are searching. New jeans will never make anyone fall in love with you; a new hair cut will not hide the pain you hold inside. Surrounding yourself with the prizes you obtain will not bring back the people you have lost; swiping that credit card one more time will not erase the pain of the past. Drinking that entire bottle calling your name in the fridge might numb your emotions and hide your fears for the night, but they will still be there in the morning. Ordering that last piece of jewelry at the amazing price on the gem network will not bring you the final peace it seems to promise you. Stuff will, in the end, be just that...stuff. Once it has lost its value, it doesn't mean a thing. Once the soles of those shoes wear out, they are not even worth keeping in your closet. Once a trinket shatters... it no longer shines.

Giving in to these gifts that attempt to promise you lasting happiness is just a temporary fix. Things of this earth will never bring you eternal happiness... only a longing for more of its temporary pleasures. Don't let the things of this world entice you into thinking that they are all you need.

When something is really broken inside... don't try to disguise it with stuff. Time after time, 'things' will try to draw you in for a temporary fix, but deep down... something is wrong. Seek to heal the parts of you that are broken... and not for things of the world that try to fill in the cracks. Even if all your stuff is taken away... the real emotion will still be there inside, trying to destroy you.

Don't spend your days walking around the Costcos and RC Willeys of the world searching for the peace you will never find inside of their walls. True peace doesn't come with a price tag and real love cannot be bought.

Christ has given us the ultimate gift. With all my heart I promise you, that *He* is the gift we must seek when we cannot find the peace for which we are searching. *He* is the light and the life of the world. *He* is the maker of eternal happiness, and only *He* holds the gifts that can help us find eternal peace. Search for the gifts that He is wrapping for all of us who have ever felt alone, who have felt we are not good enough, or that we are broken. Let His gift of love and Eternal Life bless your heart with peace.

The gift of your life has been given to you by a loving Father in Heaven, and the ultimate gift of Eternal Life has already been bought by Christ. The ultimate gift is love. Deal out His love to everyone you meet, and when you are dealt love by someone else... let it be enough.

Don't search for the love you already have right in front of you in a temporary pleasure or a new smile. Maybe you cannot feel from others the love they have for you, but for a time, pray that you will be blessed to see it... and don't let it go until you do. The pathway to eternal love and happiness will have bumps... but find a way to deal with those bumps to-gether. When the days get dark and the mountains get too hard to climb, turn toward each other, and to Jesus Christ. Any temporary excitement you find…to cover your pain…will not last. Seek for the wholesome kind of love that can last forever.

Don't wait for tragedy for your heart to be softened. Don't spend your days dealing and coping…and miss living. You have beautiful gifts of love all around you. They come in imperfect packages…but they are perfect for you. Seek to see them as He does, and someday you will be blessed to see their value. Your life is a gift, and so is every one you have been blessed to touch. The hand you have been dealt in life is yours alone…but Christ has made a deal that He will always be near.

CHAPTER THIRTY-FIVE

Enough

TIFFANIE HAD GONE HOME FOR THE WEEKEND, and I had just gotten the kids down for a nap. It was just me and a quiet house and I was almost excited to have nothing to think about. I couldn't wait to just relax and not move. I sat down to turn on the TV and turn off my brain. However, just as I found a show to watch, my phone rang. The caller ID showed it was an unknown caller.

I was disappointed to interrupt my quiet moment and I was always reluctant to answer calls from anonymous callers because my new reality meant answering random calls from all types of people, including crazies. However, I was also anxious to hear about any progress in the legal case. Everything inside of me was waiting for the trial to be over to be able to move on with my life … and any progress brought it closer to its finale.

I accepted the call, and sure enough, it was the principle detective on the case calling from the police department. "Ashlee," he said, "I have some good news. We've been waiting and waiting for the results of Emmett's blood work to come back, and they've finally come in. His blood was clean, Ashlee. There wasn't a sign of anything in his blood but those supplements you told us he was taking. There was none of the stuff the Defense has been trying to suggest he was on. Nothing. His blood was totally clean!"

I stared at the floor as he spoke. My mind raced back to that final night and the way Emmett had treated me. "Yeah … that … that's good … I just thought...he...yes. No DRUGS. That's a good thing...right? Yeah.

Thanks for letting me know. I've also been waiting to hear about the results, and it means a lot that you called to tell me yourself.....It's hard when everyone else learns about things at the same time as I do, and it's nice to hear something from you guys...before the whole town reads it in the paper and sees it on the news. So thank you. Really, I appreciate your call."

The detective let me know he would call back when any other test results came in to ease my mind about hearing the information from the police first before it was made public. I hung up the phone. Good news? Right? This *was* good news...wasn't it? Then why were my eyes burning and my heart pounding? Why was I on the verge of a meltdown?

All of the emotions I'd been bottling up about the possibility of drugs being involved came seeping out of every pour of my body. I let out a sigh filled with fear and pain...and then took a deep breath. I held it in for a few seconds as it whirled around inside of my lungs. Panic overtook my body.

I had to be certain I'd understood the detective correctly. I had to be sure! I grabbed the phone from where it had fallen to the floor and called him back. He answered, "Hey Ashlee . . .did you have another question about the results?"

I burst into tears. "Hey...no...so...what am I supposed to do now?... I...I...I just kind of hoped...that there might have been something... anything...that they found. Are you absolutely certain he hadn't been smoking pot...or that he hadn't taken some prescription pills or something? Isn't there anything? How can there be NOTHING? It just doesn't make any sense...there has to be something! Because why was he yelling at me...and why was he acting so distant? ...Why was he gone all the time?...Why was he spending time with her? ...Why didn't he want me? It had to be some type of drug...or something that was making him act that way. Why was he being so mean to me, and why wasn't I enough for him? ...I need you to tell me that you found something...so that it wasn't me he was rejecting. If he wasn't taking drugs or doing something else that was altering his thinking...then that just leaves HIM. I have nothing to blame for the reason he didn't want me. This *isn't* good news for me...like I thought it would be. If there was no sign of drugs...it means...it means he didn't want me! I can't breathe...I can't breathe...I...I...I just...I just hoped...a part of me just needed to know that there *were* drugs in his system, so *they* could be the reason he wasn't coming home. ... *They* could be what I'm mad about...and they could be what I blame when I look into the mirror tonight...all alone...and wonder WHY I wasn't enough."

"Ashlee," he replied. "I am so sorry. I...I...was just trying to help give you what I thought would be some good news for a change. ...I thought...I thought this might help you."

And that was the moment I hated Emmett. I hated everything he was, and everything he'd been in the past. I hated the fact that there weren't any drugs in his system...and that any excuses about why I hadn't been good enough for Emmett were now gone. There was no longer anything else to blame. I hated the fact that Emmett left me, and I hated that he died. I hated that he refused to see me when I was standing right there, waiting for him. I hated that every time I looked into the mirror I just saw nothing, not because I *was* nothing, but because he had treated me like I was nothing. I hated hearing his name. I hated the fact that there was a town nearby named E M M E T T, spelled just like his name to the letter. I hated that he chose to share the intimate part of our marriage with another woman. I hated the fact that that other woman had held my baby, and that he had let her! He slept with her...not because he was high on drugs...but because he wanted to! *He* did this to me...and I hated him for it.

The bitterness swelled inside of me like a sea of ice cold blood. While my babies slept soundly in their rooms, hatred filled my heart. I looked up at our mantel to the giant family portrait that graced the room. I didn't want to see his damn face. I ran over to the photo and tore it off its perch. It had no place in this room. I had no desire to stare at it any longer. I didn't want to feel him near me. I didn't want to hear his voice.

I no longer craved his presence at my side, but just in case he *was* there, I screamed at him to let him know how much I was hurting inside...and how much I hated him!

"Emmett...I know you can hear me...and I need you to listen to me right now. I didn't deserve *any* of this. YOU did this to me...and I hate you more than anything I have ever hated before. I hate your face, I hate that I gave you my heart...and that you ripped it right out of my chest. I hate that I saved myself for you, and that you spit at my feet. I hate that everything I see in this picture means NOTHING to you. You did *not* deserve us...and I hate you for making me believe that I should have shared it with you. I TRUSTED YOU! This family deserved the world, EMMETT...and our children deserved to see us live up to all the covenants and promises we made. ... They deserved to know that we believed in them! *We* created them together, Emmett, to give them a wonderful life...and you chose THIS...and I hate you for it! YOU did this to us...you brought us down...and we deserve to fly. WE didn't push you away!...We were there waiting for you. YOU chose her...her? Why weren't we worth it? ...Why...why...why wasn't I...WHY WASN'T I ENOUGH?"

After that day, I never wore my wedding ring again. As broken as I had felt before, I was now at the lowest point possible. Before that day, in the back of my mind, I truly believed Emmett must have been taking drugs and that I could blame drugs for the changes in him. It wasn't really that he didn't want me...it was that the drugs had clouded his thinking. But, that call from the detective changed everything. I could no longer blame drugs for Emmett's behavior, and that hurt more than I could have ever imagined.

In addition to never again wearing my wedding ring, I never put that family picture back up on the mantel again. The pain and anger mounting in my heart took on a whole new aspect that day. The feeling of not being enough seemed to be growing deep inside my soul. My hair began to fall out; my skin was a mess. I spent most mornings trying to push the nausea aside long enough to force myself to eat. Hatred was my constant companion, and fear was its best friend.

I remember the first time I really felt hate in my heart. I had been invited to a good friend's birthday party. She was turning eight years old. I was so excited to go and was counting down the days until the big event. One day at lunch time, on my way to recess, I stopped in the girls' bathroom and was taking my time in the stall when I heard two girls walk in. It was my friend talking about her upcoming birthday party with another girl. All of the sudden, she said in a snotty little voice, "Well...I wish I didn't have to, but my mom made me invite stupid Ashlee...so that is the only bad part...but we can still have fun."

Never in my life had I struggled with friends, and I didn't know what to say or do. I sat quietly, slowly pulling up my feet so that they wouldn't notice me inside the stall. I stayed in that bathroom the entire recess... wishing I could get that feeling of hate out of my heart. I didn't even cry... but just sat there angry that my friend was not really my friend after all. We had made so many great memories together, and I was shocked and hurt that that was how she talked about me when I wasn't there. It didn't make any sense to my little third-grade mind. Why didn't she like me? What had I done to make her not want to be with me? Why wasn't I enough for her?

Since Emmett's death, I have spent hundreds of hours asking myself those kinds of futile questions...questions that cannot be answered. Why wasn't I enough for Rob?...Wasn't the fact that I existed...another spouse suffering from the pain of infidelity...enough for him to know how badly those two bullets would impact me? Bullets....Why didn't the fact that he also had children help Rob to understand that he should have used words in their place? At the trial, I would later learn that Rob had reminded Emmett of his five children at home...just minutes before he aimed at Emmett's heart. Why didn't Rob tell that gun that it had better stay hidden...because

Emmett was a father of babies... babies who still wanted and needed him, in spite of the poor choices he was making? Why weren't *we* enough for Rob to just stay home and wait... as we were doing.

Why wasn't *I* enough for Kandi? She knew I existed. She saw the picture Emmett once proudly displayed of us. She shook my hand and looked me in the eyes. Why wasn't that picture enough for her to know that Emmett had a great life... one that had no place for her? Couldn't we have been enough for her to just stick to her job description and then go home to her own family?

These three individuals—the creators of the crossroads that destroyed my world—proved to me that I was not enough. Not one of them thought about me as they took that next step along their chosen paths. I was not worth any of their time or consideration.

To all of you who have ever felt like you were not enough for someone else, I want to share what I have come to learn in the last three years. It isn't about you. It is about the selfishness of others.

Emmett didn't cheat on me because I wasn't enough for him. ... He cheated on me because he gave in to selfish impulses. However, until I found that out for myself... I hated him because I believed it was his fault that I couldn't find myself again. Kandi didn't have an affair with my husband because she wanted to punish or hurt me. No, she only had one person in mind, and that was herself. Rob didn't stop to think about me when he reached into his pocket for that gun... because he was only thinking about himself and his own anger.

Until about four months ago, I walked around with hate permanently implanted in my heart. I dreamed about it, I cried about it, I ran from things because of it, and I couldn't let myself be fully happy... with it in my heart.

Hate will destroy you. Its power is greater than almost anything that has ever brought me down before. Hate will make you want to turn everyone else's worlds upside down... merely to make their views match your own. Hate will take hold of your heart...and it will try to ruin you.

My hate was a REACTION to the selfishness around me, and not an ACTION that I intentionally chose.

We must learn that there will be explosions in our faces. In one way or another, there will not be anyone who lives in this world who will not suffer from one of life's nasty blasts. What I wish I had known before having to walk down the aisles of the school of hard knocks, is that I could have chosen to stand. But I know it now. I *can* stand. I can stand against hate. I can leave no place for it in my heart. I can stand against the actions of others. I do *not* have to react to anyone else's choices, or words. I can stand in the truths that I know. I can stand even when others' selfishness tries to pull me down.

Sometimes—because of the selfishness of others—the answer that is the most difficult to find is to the question: AM I ENOUGH? The damage others may cause us leaves a pain that is hard to console. At times, we are left not only with the fear that we are alone...but with the belief that we were not worth fighting for...that we were not enough.

However, the truth that can prove us wrong in our thinking is always close by. There is a message of hope that we can all seek, and it will teach us what is real:

I am enough, for myself...and I am enough for God.

Everything else, well...frankly doesn't really matter. Husbands may cheat; wives may leave. Bosses may fire employees; children may mock. Strangers may steal; neighbors may offend. Spouses may die, and tragedies may come . . .but even after the dust settles...you are still you. No person or event can take that away from you or determine who you will become.

The selfishness of others may make you feel as if you are being thrown into a pack of wolves...and you may feel like you are all alone with just a stick with which to fight them off. But...YOU ARE NOT ALONE. The wolves may snap at you. They may even take a bite out of your heart...

without a second thought as to how it might affect you. They may slink away, leaving you to die alone, or they may howl out to the world that you weren't enough for them. You may be left with nothing but your insecurities and despair... and even after the blood dries and the wounds close... their voices might still echo in your heart. They may even howl each night at the moon... and you may wonder if it is your nothingness that they continue to shriek about. Their powerful wails may be heard for years to come... but their lies do *not* have to define who you view yourself to be.

I have two words for you about all the wolves in the world who have tried or continue to try to bring you down: who cares? It doesn't matter. They don't matter. Even if you are standing alone... at least you are not falling into the darkness with them.

Their cries may be overpowering... but you do not have to listen. You may feel the darkness as their howling seeks you out... but you can move back into the light. You will be presented with many reasons to doubt yourself and Satan will keep sending the wolves... over and over to convince you of the worthlessness of your soul... but you can remember who you really are. The wolves may claw at your door every hour of every day... but you can FIGHT.

Satan does not own you, and he hates you for that, but he will continue to send selfishness and hate to consume you. He will send packs of wolves to try to rip you to shreds. FIGHT.

And don't stop fighting.

You *are* enough. I *was* enough then... and I am enough now. I have to tell myself that every single day. I am not alone, and I am worth dying for. Emmett may not have died fighting for me, but Jesus Christ did.

Every time I want to just give up, and every moment I focus on the fact that Emmett was shot fighting for her... darkness envelopes me. All the months I let those thoughts fester and focused on my pain... I was literally eaten alive and consumed by hatred. Once I realized that my pain wasn't worth living with, and that my hatred was not allowing me to breath...I felt free. The only way I was going to live through it...was by letting it go.

I fight the darkness now when it surrounds me. I try hard not to let it find a corner inside my heart for even a second. When I feel it come, I immediately get down on my knees and pray for Christ's light. I have felt Him send Angels to take my pain back to Him. He promised He would carry me when I could not stand alone...and He has. He died for me because I *was* enough, and He wants me to live for Him...because He is all I need. He is enough for me.

He wants each of us to know that we are worth dying for. He wants us to know that He loves us. He wants us to fight to be on His side. His way does not always come easily...especially when we have made a home for hatred in our hearts. When the "good news" of the world brings you to your knees in pain...Christ is the only one who can help you let go of the hate in your heart. The world will tell you that His way is not enough. It will promise you a life full of passion and excitement and lead you to believe that you deserve better than the simple life you are living. The world will try to convince you that it isn't enough. The world is wrong.

You are the perfect creation of a perfect Heavenly Father. He sent His Son to die for you...because you *are* enough for Him.

CHAPTER THIRTY-SIX

Crossroads Collide

THE NIGHT EMMETT WAS MURDERED I FOUND myself standing at a crossroad. A fork had been thrown into the road of the life that I loved by three other people. Emmett was gone, Rob was in jail, and Kandi was not a person who could have comforted me.

Crossroads. The one thing that is constant in our lives is change. Most of the time, we come to these crossroads…unprepared to make the big decisions about which path to take.

The crossroads that collided with mine that night left me alone to choose how I would handle my own. This life is going to be hard. It is going to test and try us each and every day.

So, what if every fear you have ever tried to avoid finds you…all in one night? You may lose your ability to breath for a time, you may struggle to find your purpose for a long while…but you are still *you*. You are still strong, you are still important, and you are still loveable.

Since that dreadful event, there has not been a day that has gone by when I haven't questioned a part of myself. I have learned that there will always be darkness that will try to destroy us. Each and every day is a test, but each day is also a gift.

There is beauty all around us. There is light at the end of every dark tunnel. I have found it, woven in around my pain. I have seen it creep in silently as I was surrounded by darkness: a song sung just for me, a speaker whose words felt like they were written to heal my heart, a whisper to my soul through the power of my dreams. Beauty doesn't ever come in perfection, but in subtle glimpses through imperfect people and circumstances.

This world may feel heavy, some nights may be dark…but I choose to stand. I choose to stand in my faith; I choose to stand in my family; I choose to stand with my God; and I choose to stand in who I am.

Life is not over until it is over. We will be wronged. We will make mistakes. The silence in our hearts may break because of the evil of this world, but the darkness can never break us. It can destroy the life we thought we knew, it can try to pull us down…but we have the power to turn darkness into victory. When we choose to stand with God, even when the silence breaks…He will never let us fall.

Some days you might not be able to put your feet on the ground, but God will be there to help you stand, if you truly seek Him. If you truly want to stand in moments of difficulty, you must make Him a part of your story.

We all have stories to tell. This is my story, but this is only the beginning. My children still had challenges to overcome. I still had a new life to forge, a trial to get through, and healing and forgiveness to complete. I still had many moments to come where I would need God's help to stand. And my goal…was to stand tall through it all.